StyleCity
LONDON

StyleCity

LONDON

Harry N. Abrams, Inc., Publishers

Contents

Street Wise

Style Traveller

Specially commissioned photography by
Ingrid Rasmussen and Anthony Webb

Series concept and editor: Lucas Dietrich
Texts: Phyllis Richardson
Original design concept and maps: The Senate
Jacket and book design: Grade Design Consultants

Although every effort has been made to ensure that the information in this book is as up-to-date and as accurate as possible at the time of going to press, some details are liable to change.

All prices listed in this guide are quoted in the local currency.

Library of Congress Cataloging-in-Publication Data

StyleCity London: a select guide for the discerning global traveler.
        p.   cm.—(StyleCity)
ISBN 0 8109-9107-1 (pbk. with flaps)
1. London (England)—Guidebooks. I. Harry N. Abrams, Inc.
II. Series.

DA679.S896 2003
914.2104'86—dc21

                                    2002156273

Printed and bound in China
10 9 8 7 6 5 4 3 2

Harry N. Abrams, Inc.
100 Fifth Avenue
New York, N.Y. 10011
www.abramsbooks.com

Abrams is a subsidiary of

LA MARTINIÈRE
GROUPE

How to Use This Guide

The book features two principal sections: **Street Wise** and **Style Traveller**.

    Street Wise, which is arranged by neighbourhood, features areas that can be covered in a day (and night) on foot and includes a variety of locations – cafés, shops, restaurants, museums, performace spaces, bars – that capture local flavour or are lesser-known destinations.

    The establishments in the **Style Traveller** section represent the city's best and most characteristic locations – 'worth a detour' – and feature hotels (**sleep**), restaurants (**eat**), cafés and bars (**drink**), boutiques and shops (**shop**) and getaways (**retreat**).

    Each location is shown as a circled number on the relevant neighbourhood map, which is intended to provide a rough idea of location and proximity to major sights and landmarks rather than precise position. Locations in each neighbourhood are presented sequentially by map number. Each entry in the **Style Traveller** has two numbers: the top one refers to the page number of the neighbourhood map on which it appears; the second number is its location.

For example, the visitor might begin by selecting a hotel from the **Style Traveller** section. Upon arrival, **Street Wise** might lead him to the best joint for coffee before guiding him to a house-museum nearby. After lunch he might go to find a special jewelry store listed in the **shop** section. For a memorable dining experience, he might consult his neighbourhood section to find the nearest restaurant crossreferenced to **eat** in **Style Traveller**.

    Street addresses are given in each entry, and complete information – including email and web addresses – is listed in the alphabetical **contact** section. Travel and contact details for the destinations in **retreat** are given at the end of **contact**.

Legend

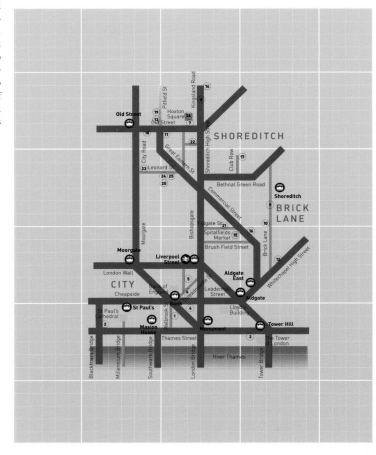

- **(2)** Location
- Museums, sights
- Squares, markets
- Tube stops
- Principal street
- Secondary road

LONDON

Like many cosmopolises, London is heterogeneous and multilayered, complex and contradictory. According to a 2000 United Nations census, London's greater metropolitan area included
around seven and a half million inhabitants, making it the 26th largest city in the world. Although
it may not be one of the globe's top ten most populous cities, it is arguably the most diverse
and among the most culturally influential. Bridging the United States and Europe in many, often
conflicting, ways, and being the capital city on an island, as opposed to a continent, have impart-
ed to London a number of curious qualities that have often insulated it from (if not made it
resist) the larger continental forces across the Atlantic and the English Channel.

Intensified by a dense historic urban fabric that has been fractured by the Great Fire
of 1666 and the Second World War, London's political, cultural and social spheres have a potent
way of intersecting and mixing. Unlike many larger European cities, which have grown concen-
trically out from a historic (usually medieval) centre of power, and American cities (except
Los Angeles), which are based on the democratic grid, London is a concatenation of essentially autonomous villages that have merged over time. What were once royal hunting grounds in
the 17th century or new suburbs in the 19th have been subsumed into the greater whole that
is London today.

The result of this is that London has not one heart but many. With the exception of the
Mall, London is unmarked by the grand urban gestures of Pope Sixtus V's Rome, Haussmann's
Paris or Cerda's Barcelona, which created axes rather than centres. London's composition of
mainly smaller streets and lanes feels distinctly unmodern, unimposing and accessible – a
pedestrian paradise. Whereas most visitors regard the main tourist sights – Trafalgar Square,
Buckingham Palace, St Paul's Cathedral – as central London, for Londoners there is no true
centre, except perhaps the high street of their neighbourhood. There are financial centres (the
City) and cultural magnets (the West End), but in the main London is everywhere. The best way
to experience everyday London is in its villages.

The millennium has seen an efflorescence of *grands projets* in the capital, which has
revivified the worlds of the arts, design and fashion and substantiated the 'Cool Britannia'
image beyond the media. Perhaps the most successful and popular of these recent catalysts is

Tate Modern (p. 104), which has awakened the British populace's largely guarded attitude towards contemporary art, provided visitors to the city with a genuinely modern cultural destination and stimulated a neglected part of London, the South Bank. Moreover, there are less-publicized but equally important cultural institutions that are enjoying new leases of life: the intimate National Portrait Gallery has now been significantly expanded with a new wing (which includes a restaurant providing unparalleled views over the city; see p. 148). The Royal Opera House (p. 54) has been refurbished, enlarged, modernized and incorporated into a lively tourist destination, the Covent Garden Piazza. The British Museum has been restored to its original 19th-century form and given a Great Court by architect Norman Foster's canopy of glass. Somerset House (p. 57) has been reinvented and restored and its several major art collections brought back to life. A number of smaller museums, often overlooked by visitors to the city, have also been renewed and extended since 2000: the Wallace Collection in Marylebone (p. 64), for example, enjoys a new atrium designed by Rick Mather.

But perhaps no buildings symbolize the city's optimism and 21st-century outlook more than the Greater London Authority (G.L.A.) building, also by Foster, and the London Eye, designed by Julie Barkow and David Marks, on London's South Bank. With their curvilinear forms on prominent riverside positions and their manifest high technology and transparency, these buildings signal London's openness to modernity and new forms of expression.

Yet, while the face of London may be enjoying a public restoration, the most dynamic element of the city remains its thriving, though less visible underground scene. New trends in music, fashion and art that gain global popularity are often the product of London's subcultures rather than its established institutions. At the turn of the millennium, London images of 'street style' have as much influence on the world as they did in the 1960s. Inspired by an edgy, vital youth culture and the broad spectrum of ethnic influences, London's creative scene continues to confirm the city's position as a world leader.

As with any great city, it is impossible to distil London's essence; even life-long inhabitants are unable to characterize the city's complexity, to reconcile what is English versus what is international. But London thrives on the very contradictions it creates, the borders that it blurs. Visitors wishing to experience London beyond its tourist destinations will begin to discover its idiosyncrasies, its uniqueness and its timeless appeal in the places that follow.

Street Wise

Notting Hill • Holland Park • Kensington • Knightsbridge •
Chelsea • Mayfair • Soho • Covent Garden • Marylebone • Fitzrovia •
Bloomsbury • Holborn • Clerkenwell • Islington • King's Cross • City •
Shoreditch • Brick Lane • South Bank • Southwark • Bermondsey

Notting Hill
Holland Park
Kensington

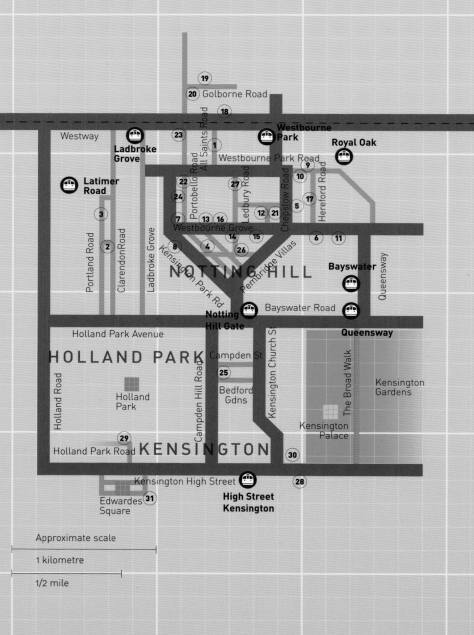

Westway

Ladbroke Grove

(19)

(20) Golborne Road

(18)

Westbourne Park

Royal Oak

(23)

All Saints Road

(1)

Westbourne Park Road

Latimer Road

(3)

Portobello Road

(22)

(24)

(27)

Ledbury Road

(9)

(10)

Chepstow Road

(17)

(5)

Hereford Road

Portland Road

ClarendonRoad

Ladbroke Grove

(2)

(7)

(13) (16)

(12) (21)

Westbourne Grove

(8)

(4)

(14)

(15)

(26)

(6)

(11)

N O T T I N G   H I L L

Kensington Park Rd

Pembridge Villas

Bayswater

Queensway

Notting Hill Gate

Bayswater Road

Queensway

Holland Park Avenue

HOLLAND PARK

Campden St

Kensington Church St

The Broad Walk

Kensington Gardens

Holland Road

Campden Hill Road

(25)

Bedford Gdns

Holland Park

Kensington Palace

(29)

KENSINGTON

Holland Park Road

(30)

Kensington High Street

(28)

High Street Kensington

Edwardes Square

(31)

Approximate scale

1 kilometre

1/2 mile

Walking around the designer-label shops and trendy cafés of Notting Hill today, you would never suspect that as late as the 1950s this was one of London's most impoverished areas, nor would you immediately suspect that it is the centre for the city's Afro-Caribbean culture. The latter distinction is celebrated every August Bank Holiday weekend, when the Notting Hill Carnival swings into gear and around two million people pour into W11 and W2 for days and nights of colourful pageantry, dance music and street-fair fun. When its gentrification began some years ago, Notting Hill became known as the home of 'Trustafarians' (trust fund + Rastafarian), those twenty- and thirty-somethings who emerged from their privileged backgrounds and/or private schools in search of a kind of bohemia, albeit luxurious. So, although gradually regenerated over the past decades and brought into the world's public consciousness by a movie starring Julia Roberts and Hugh Grant, Notting Hill represents a determined effort to preserve the air of arty-funky lifestyle.

Fortunately for year-round visitors, the carnival atmosphere epitomized by the Notting Hill Carnival can be experienced more than once a year. Every weekend the antiques market on Portobello Road, the area's spiritual and geographic backbone, adds a suitable dash of gritty urbanism and multicultural vibe while providing useful hunks of old Victoriana, with enough wear and tear to make it obvious they didn't come from the grandparents' manor house. Shops and pubs lining the north end of Portobello Road represent the new blood in Notting Hill in terms of talent and artistic edge. All Saints Road, once known for its laid-back, drug-induced groove, is today an almost idyllic enclave, with street-smart eating, drinking and shopping all along a couple of blocks. Some of the area's more adventuresome places are around the junction of Westbourne Grove and Needham Road; whereas the convergence of Westbourne Grove and Ledbury Road is a smorgasbord of new-era designers, galleries and eateries that could easily hold you in thrall for an afternoon.

Farther south, the largely residential and seriously upscale areas of Holland Park and Kensington need little introduction. The quarter's centrepiece is Holland Park itself, providing one of those grand oases of green space in which London rejoices. Whereas so many localities of London are famous – or infamous – for their energy and verve, Kensington is the pure embodiment of English gentility, urban-style, but, like so many of the capital's neighbourhoods, just another village.

1 All Saints Road
- The Pelican, no. 45
- Trudy Hanson, no. 25
- Uli, no. 16
- Zig Zag, no. 12
- Manor, no. 6
- The Jacksons, no. 5

Mixing Notting Hill off-beat funky with more upscale tendencies, All Saints Road, a two-block enclave and a short distance from the touristy Portobello Market, is a microcosm of the best of west London. Anchoring one end of the street is the organic pub-restaurant the Pelican, with inviting globe lanterns hanging outside and a colourful, warm and friendly pub inside, with dining on the first floor. Dishes are innovative British cuisine, organic being no hindrance to variety. Since she set up shop in 1994, Trudy Hanson has aimed to make 'modern, simple bridal wear' that is 'cut to flatter'. She's now produced her elegant, smooth-fitting designs for more than 1000 women. Zig Zag is one of the street's groovy bars, which you'll know by its bold red walls and equally vibrant crowd; a different but equally hip nightspot is Manor. Much-loved English retro-hip designers The Jacksons have a white-painted corner shop full of highly coveted shoes, bags, scarves and belts. Thai-Chinese restaurant Uli is an acclaimed neighbourhood gem with the added surprise of a garden in the back.

FLOWER POWER
2 Cath Kidston
8 Clarendon Cross

British textile designer Cath Kidston's Notting Hill shop is a bower of bright prints and flowers in a distinctly crisp English style that has been much praised for its witty and nostalgic appeal. Floral patterns in reds, blues and yellows, as well as bold polka dots and stripes, are splashed across everything, from aprons to ironing board covers, pillows to tablecloths. With a hint of vintage that manages to stay the tasteful side of kitsch, each item is finely finished, but for those seeking to make their own statement, there are also bolts of fabrics available.

ROAD TO FASHION

3   Portland Road
- Julie's, no. 135
- Virginia, no. 98
- The Cross, no. 141

Portland Road becomes a villagey collection at Notting Hill's north end, which provides a taste of stylish neighbourhood life. Virginia attracts vintage addicts from all over London with its collection of lacey Victorian and latter-day delicates. Its straw hats and flowers are mirrored by the romantic conservatory seating at Julie's across the way, a restaurant that has long been a favourite with the locals and features themed rooms soaked in candlelight by night. Up the road a little farther you'll find another destination for London designers and celebrities. As well as carrying new British designer clothing, The Cross sells those little accessories that speak volumes in fashion language.

SOUTH AMERICAN FUSION

4   Wall
1 Denbigh Road

Peruvian Hernan Balcazar and his British-born wife, Judith, have brought the riches of Andean fabrics to London with inventive flair. As creative director, Judith Balcazar works with in-house designers to create a range of women's clothing that is comfortable as daywear and elegant enough for the evening. From simple T-shirts to linen jackets and alpaca coats, the pieces signify 'simplicity, luxury and comfort'. Using special blends of handpicked cotton, alpaca and vicuña, the pieces tend towards neutrals in summer and warm contrasts in winter, such as dark cinnamon and cherry.

LEATHER LUXE

5   Bill Amberg
170

A bright new-style Indian restaurant, Ginger, that will make you stop and stare over its silvery booths and turquoise chairs. Another reason to stop is that its kitchen genius, Albert Gomes, was head chef at one of Bangladesh's most luxurious hotels and his aim is to bring speciality Bangladeshi food, not just the umbrella Indian style, to London. Fried red pumpkin, duck and mango curry and Bengali fishcakes are just some of the unusual and wonderfully prepared dishes that cover the range of fish, seafood, chicken, lamb and a particularly lauded biryani.

Nadia Demetriou Ladas's Notting Hill tableware shop and gallery is the result of an obsession. Ladas began collecting 1950s glassware after visiting the glass-blowing region of southern Sweden and developed a collecting habit that, she says, 'became a joke' among her friends. Today her commitment to contemporary design is evident in the Scandinavian pieces, Italian art glass and works by such important British designers as Tom Dixon and Nigel Coates and sculptor Anish Kapoor. 'Everything in the shop has been chosen with passio', she explains, and 'all fit into Walter Gropius's definition of good design, that they should have beauty, quality, function and affordability'. The shop was designed by Ladas's partner, furniture designer Angel Monzon. During non-exhibition periods, visitors can use the downstairs space to browse magazines while enjoying a cup of jasmine tea.

The Westbourne is one of those places that looks so inviting and appealing that trying to resist a swift half is futile. Perhaps it's the outdoor terrace, usually filled with youthful locals, or the quiet, tree-lined setting somewhat removed from the area's buzzier streets. A reincarnation of an old neighbourhood boozer, with large forecourt and wood-filled interiors, it boasts a modern menu and attractive clientele that are happy to be in the know.

Opened in 1999 to 'showcase the best of British contemporary applied arts', Flow was established by Yvonna Demczynska, who had worked as a dealer in British crafts in the U.S. and Japan. With an interior that is clever but not overwhelming, the work of the gallery's 40 represented artists, working in ceramics, glass, wood, textiles, basketry, metal and jewelry, displayed atop floating white shelves. Of particular recent interest are works in 'hot glass' by British graduates: Keiko Mukaide's 'garden of 30 glass plants', Amy Cushing's pieces incorporating materials developed in the space programme or Bob Durlington's cool-coloured, sensuous forms.

'Sensual bed-linen and seduction wear and lifestyle luxuries' is how Space Boudoir describes the satiny, plush range of bedding, pyjamas and indulgent little accessories they produce. The shop started with an artistic focus and well-chosen art works still dot the plush, fairy-lit premises, but the boudoir emphasis, which used to be a section of the range, has taken over, and rightfully so, as these pieces shouldn't languish anywhere but against the skin. Quilted, hand-stitched satin blankets and silk lounging pyjamas

are just the start to the boudoir experience. Designer Emma Oldham's penchant for luxury extends to aroma and trinkets as well.

Up a quiet street from humming Westbourne Grove, Mission is just that: a dedication to an ideal. The recently redesigned shop/gallery/exhibition reflects a holistic view of art, supporting the goal to 'nurture the senses'. The sculpted backdrop, as well as the furnishings, objects, ceramics and lighting, resonate with purity of form. Modern designs by Ou Baholydhin, Patrick Fredikson and Michael Wolfson sit in beautiful composition with pieces dating as far back as the 1940s. You will need to phone ahead.

A spacious young bar at the top end of the Portobello market's gamut of stalls, the Bed Bar is as relaxing as it sounds. Traditional wobbly wood chairs have been thrown out in favour of large banquettes covered in brightly upholstered cushions. Downstairs, lounging is encouraged, while upstairs, proper tables and a separate cocktail bar invite more involved conversations. The atmosphere is casual and the service upbeat. A good place to while away an afternoon with a pint or sprawl out of an evening.

21 Miller Harris
14 Needham Road

Lyn Harris is the young perfumer behind this very highly regarded line. After working with perfume-makers in Paris and Grasse, she launched her own range with the help of perfume house Robertet, who helps manufacture her very distinctive collection. Basing many of her perfumes on 'old-fashioned, naturally derived' aromas, which are more expensive to work with than synthetics, she creates complex concoctions such as 'Coeur Fleur', a mix of sweet pea, mimosa, Egyptian jasmine, raspberry, peach, Florentine iris, amber and Madagascan vanilla. The beautifully designed shop also houses her scent garden, 'full of roses, jasmine and herbs', which customers are encouraged to visit. Harris offers a bespoke service consultancy, inviting clients to access her fragrance library and laboratory to create their own personal fragrances. Look sharp, though, as this service is currently booked more than six months in advance. This is the only Miller Harris shop and carries limited edition fragrances, such as 'Incense', which she created with designer Matthew Williamson, that are not available anywhere else.

ANTIQUES AND BRIC-A-BRAC
22 Portobello Road

One of London's most popular street markets, Portobello Road has evolved from its late-19th-century association with gypsies' trading horses, and is today known for its stalls of antique furnishings, prints and accessories that attract tourists and collectors from the around the world. Some of the stalls are offshoots of existing shops, but a good many are independent, with quality varying from real finds to those with more than a fair share of whimsy. The market is also full of clothing, music and a jumble of other items. It's perhaps the carnival atmosphere that is most appealing and only happens on Saturday (though shops are open six days a week). A very pleasant way to pass the morning and perhaps uncover a treasure or two.

YOUNG AND INSPIRED
23 Portobello Green
281 Portobello Road
• Preen, no. 5
• Puppy, no. 26
• Baby Ceylon, no. 16
• Zarvis, no. 4

Under the cover of the Westway flyover an arcade of small boutiques with the unlikely appellation of Portobello Green is tucked away off the busy Portobello Road. There is not much green here, but there are plenty of other colours to attract you among the array of young designers. The fanned and pleated new Victorian-style designs of Preen, for example, have attracted a celebrity following, while Puppy produces bright graphic and photo-print bed-linens and pillows; Baby Ceylon has womenswear in softer floral patterns and pastels. Be prepared to be drawn in to Zarvis, whose cornucopia of scented oils, salts and body treatments fragrantly overflows with temptation.

ALL MOD CONS
24 The Electric Cinema
191 Portobello Road

Already a London institution for movie mavens, the Electric has made itself even more popular with a recent refurbishment by Nick Jones, the man behind members-club Soho House and the artful Babington House near Bath (see p. 180). An amazing glass frontage conceals a feat of restoration and refinement that has resulted in marvellously comfortable leather armchairs with footstools and tables to hold your movie snacks in the theatre. There is also an updated bar, open half an hour before screenings and serving wine, beer, champagne and cocktails, as well as 'substantial cinema snacks'. It all adds up to one of the most comfortable and satisfying nights you will ever have at the pictures and one that is full of atmosphere even before the film starts rolling. Originally opened in 1910, the cinema was modelled on the design of old music halls, and the restoration retains the detailed plasterwork, vaulted ceiling with gilded highlights and Edwardian entryway.

PLEASING DECAY
25 Windsor Castle
155

DREAMY DRAPERY
26 Ghost
175

NEIGHBOURHOOD CHARM
27 Ledbury Road

- Duchamp, no. 75
- Blenheim Books, 11 Blenheim Crescent
- Simon Finch, no. 61A
- Wild at Heart, no. 49A

Ledbury Road is a fulcrum of the Notting Hill scene that has managed to retain its charm with a parade of small, idiosyncratic shops. Mitchell Jacobs at Duchamp was an early resident on this designers' row. He specializes in men's dress shirts, ties, cufflinks and socks with decided flair. Jacobs has a real penchant for strong colour, so you will find candy-coloured shirts in three different cuff designs (casino, double and two-button) paired with ties full of texture and bright, contrasting hues in modern patterns. Geometric, jewel-set cufflinks add the finishing sartorial touch.

Simon Finch has been trading in antique and second-hand books since his university days. This shop, opened in 1999, demonstrates the success of his commitment with a techno-modern design by Marina Chan of AMP that displays his collection of 20th-century literature and photography titles. His earlier shop on Maddox Street in Mayfair still brims with the wide range of his stock.

Farther down, you'll be struck by the equally eye-catching combinations at Wild at Heart, a flower shop whose design by Future Systems is as lively as its blossoms. Nikki Tibbles likes putting flowers in bold bunches with blooms sorted in shades and contrasts cheek by jowl. The daisy-yellow sofas and shiny white display banks would stop you even if it weren't for the beautiful floral concoctions. If you want to start your own version of Eden, there is help near by. Blenheim Books is an expert source for books on everything relating to the green arts, from planting to landscape design.

INDIAN CUISINE REIMAGINED
28 Zaika

143

29 Leighton House Museum

12 Holland Park Road

Behind the brick façade of the former studio-house of the high Victorian artist Frederic Lord Leighton (1830–96) is a spectacular paean to 19th-century decoration and craftsmanship with an exotic Eastern flavour that was popular among Leighton's artistic circle. Truly an extraordinary building, it was begun in 1864, and Leighton took up residence two years later and continued with the embellishment until his death. Among the house's many treasures are several contributions from some of the great talents of the period, including perhaps the finest collection of tiles by William de Morgan and a theatrical Arab Hall complete with fountain, elaborate mosaic floor, cupola and stained glass. The collections feature many of Leighton's meticulous drawings and some of his paintings, as well as others by such contemporaries as Edward Burne-Jones, John Everett Millais and George Frederick Watts.

TIMELESS CLASSIC
30 Maggie Jones

6 Old Court Place

In the face of the epicurian revolution that has taken hold in London over the past decade, Maggie Jones's menu, which has changed little over 40 years, is something of an institution. Thankfully, this has less to do with tradition and more to do with how reliably good the food is. Prawn cocktail, avocado and smoked chicken for starters and fish pie and poached salmon are among the regulars on the menu, with specials that change daily. Three floors of rough wood tables and high-backed settles make cosy dining on the busiest evenings, which are common. Crowds are part of the charm of Maggie Jones, along with the fresh flowers, colourful funky crockery and well-worn wood furniture. It's hard not to feel comfortable here.

AGEING GRACEFULLY
31 The Scarsdale Tavern

23A Edwardes Square

In one of Kensington's most exclusive neighbourhoods, less than a minute from Kensington High Street and filled with bright-white Georgian terraced houses draped with purple wisteria, is an enchanting public house with a façade that looks straight from the chocolate box. No commercial reproduction this – it's an age-old favourite of the well-heeled locals who savour the good food and quiet, homey atmosphere.

Knightsbridge
Chelsea

27 Serpentine Gallery

Hyde Park

Park Lane

Kensington Road

Kensington Road

Green Park

26 Knightbridge

16 Hyde Park Corner

Buckingham Palace

Royal Albert Hall

Exhibition Rd

Brompton Road

Kinnerton St

Wilton St

15

Victoria & Albert Museum

Beaufort Gdns

8

25

Grosvenor Place

Natural History Museum

Beauchamp Pl

1

7

Cromwell Road

South Kensington

13

22

21 Pont Street

K N I G H T S B R I D G E

Old Brompton Road

5

Walton Street

Sloane Street

Fulham Road

4

Ellis Street

23

Eaton Square

Elizabeth St

20

19

Victoria

9

Sydney Street

Cadogan Gardens

24

28

10

Old Church Street

Sloane Square

18

17

14

Sloane Square

CHELSEA

6

King's Road

2

11

Pimlico Road

3

Royal Hospital Road

Chelsea Embankment

12

Chelsea Physic Garden

River Thames

Buckingham Palace Road

Approximate scale

1 kilometre

1/2 mile

With the vast lush green expanse of Hyde Park to the north and the gleaming Chelsea Embankment to the south, the largely residential areas of Chelsea and Knightsbridge are probably the most picturesque and stereotypically preserved areas of London. Chelsea's immaculate terraced houses dripping with purple wisteria in the summer and Knightsbridge's high-end shopping create a patch of what can only be described as incredibly civilized London.

The spirit and symbol of Knightsbridge for most visitors is Harrod's, which still holds a certain cachet as a purveyor of luxury and designer-brand goods. For locals, however, it is the smaller, more intensively stylish department store Harvey Nichols, at the top of Sloane Street, which emerged during the 1990s as the vanguard of the younger set whose parents shopped at Harrod's. Rather than providing the feeling of a grand old country-house larder, Harvey Nichols's upstairs food hall was contemporary and sleek.

Harrod's and Harvey Nichols might reflect the tension between tradition and modernity that gives so many parts of London their edginess, but Knightbridge's creative side is driven by the presence of the Victoria and Albert Museum (p. 29), whose magnificent collections have ensured that the surrounding area has what must be one of the highest concentrations of fabric and upholstery stores and interior designers in the world. Although the character of much of the area's design remains at the traditional end, there are clear signs that attitudes are changing: the design by radical architect Daniel Libeskind and structural engineering wizard Cecil Balmond for a contorted 'spiral' addition to the V & A has been passed by the local authorities, and a team of young curators are presenting ever more exciting exhibitions. Increasing globalization has brought modernity to classic sensibilities in the interior decoration realm as well – Kit Kemp's Knightsbridge Hotel (p. 116) and David Collins's Blue Bar (p. 150) are great recent examples.

Ever since the King's Road made a splash in the 1970s, Chelsea's shops and designers continue to present their particularly English take on high style and fashion. The shops along Sloane Street are dominated by predictable global fashion labels, so those seeking funkier boutiques and more adventurous outlets should head to King's and Fulham Roads. But seek out the smaller streets, like antiques-shop-lined Walton Street, Beauchamp Place (p. 32) or Pont Street (p. 37), because they capture Chelsea's charming character and the quintessence of classical – or modern-traditional – English design more than anywhere else in the capital.

GARDENS OF DELIGHT

1 The Victoria and Albert Museum

Cromwell Road

The largest museum of applied and decorative arts in the world needs little introduction. You might see only one collection – 'Clothing through History' in the Dress Gallery, for example or the splendours of the Asian and Islamic Art collection. You might spend a lot of time staring at the Great Bed of Ware in the grand, recently refurbished and not-to-be-missed British Galleries (1500–1900) – with pieces by Chippendale, Morris, Mackintosh, Wedgwood and Liberty – or Lord Leighton's frescoes after having visited his astonishing house (p. 25) or the magical Glass Gallery. Whatever you manage to see, no visit should be without a stroll through the Pirelli Garden, an Italian-style piazza garden set within the late-19th-century walled courtyard. A large central fountain gurgles beneath grand, swaying trees, and in summer a tented enclosure serves refreshments and visitors can enjoy the garden and museum until 10 pm on Wednesdays.

HISTORIC REPRODUCTIONS

2 William Yeoward Crystal

336 King's Road

British glass designer William Yeoward set up this sparkling shop on Chelsea's King's Road in 1996 with the ingenious idea of creating reproduction English Georgian (18th century) crystal for purchase off the shelf or by special order. Stem- and barware, jugs, decanters, plates and vases are all handblown and handcut to historic patterns, many in fine floral designs. Yeoward also presents a refreshingly modern take on reproduction tableware, with a bright-looking purple shop and prices that range from an unintimidating £25 for a hand-crafted wine glass.

THE FINEST POINT

3 Manolo Blahnik

163

LOBSTER LANGOS
COD HADDOCK
MONK TURBOT H
DOVER/LEMONSOL
MACKEREL BASS
SALMON DRESS
CHERRYSTONE C
PALOURDES MUS
KINGPRAWNS PL
LOBSTER SALE
SATURDAY
SMK FISH AVAIL

AL FRESCO OYSTERS AND CHAMPAGNE

4 Bibendum Oyster Bar

Michelin House, 81 Fulham Road

Designer and entrepreneur Terence Conran has been an influential part of the British restaurant scene ever since he opened his Soup Kitchens in the 1950s. Design and food have combined in a number of widely publicized restaurant ventures (some happier than others) by the design guru, but one of his earlier – and most lasting – eateries is located in the Art Nouveau Michelin Tyre headquarters (architecturally interesting in its own right). While upstairs is the formal Bibendum restaurant, the ground floor features an informal seafood bar and restaurant serving a wide variety of oysters, caviar and *fruits de la mer*, in a patio-like setting next to a bright flower stall.

INDULGENCES

5 Bentleys

172

WELL-DRESSED AND SO TO BED

6 Couverture

310 King's Road

Emily Dyson says that her signature is in the detail, rather than in the grand design, and that is what catches the eye at Couverture, a shop opened in 1999 and dedicated to well-designed bedclothes and bed-linens. Formerly a designer concerned with detailing for British fashion leader Paul Smith, Dyson identified a gap in the market for the kind of finely trimmed linens you might associate with antique or vintage articles, and then presented them with a thoroughly modern attitude. While the shop is awash with white and pale shades, closer inspection reveals a velvet cuff on a silk pyjama bottom or dressing gown or a needlework-patterned hem on sheets and pillow-cases that impart that satisfying – if not totally soporific – hint of luxury. Couverture also carries a small number of quirky items by designers selected by Dyson, so tiny, hand-tied dolls or bright children's sneakers pop up around the displays of luxurious satins and silks.

A street of genuine luxury, Beauchamp Place is worth a visit just to stroll by and admire the dazzling shop windows of purveyors of haute couture like Bruce Oldfield and Isabell Kristensen to peek in at the jewellers Dower & Hall, who have their workshop upstairs. There is also a branch of Royal English perfumer Penhaligon's, which offers beauty treatments on the premises; and lingerie legend Janet Reger, who has produced supremely seductive intimate apparel since the 1960s for everyone from Joan Collins to Nicole Kidman and Madonna, beckons from no. 10. Irish designer Paul Costelloe's latest collection features wonderfully minimal separates, and a few of his recent tableware designs for Wedgwood are on display. Sitting somewhat incongruously amid high fashions is the Map House, a source of fine antique maps, globes and engravings for almost a century. Try a drink at Townhouse, a new boutique restaurant and bar.

Simon Wilson has been designing costume jewelry for over 25 years, and some of his better-known pieces are creatures – the 'lazy lizard', 'slinky serpent' and 'friendly spider'. But there are also the delicate drop earrings and pendants in soft pastels, gems that are displayed alongside the shop's array of vintage items, which includes a selection of antique Scottish jewelry, Art Déco pieces in silver, semiprecious stones and marcasite and a treasure trove of one-off bags – beaded, box-shaped and zippered. A recent refurbishment, with a retro-looking turquoise wash, means the shop leaps out of the upmarket boutiques of the Fulham Road, promising something inviting and altogether more fun.

Designer Tricia Guild's King's Road mecca for vivid and contemporary home furnishings and fabrics stocks an array of objects from furnishings to greeting cards, but what makes her place so appealing, apart from the Mediterranean colours that mark her collections, is that every piece is the work of a named designer or craftsperson. Since 1970 she has been amassing the work of artisans, from abroad and locally, to create an exceptionally vibrant selection, a breath of fresh air in a design scene dominated by grey modernistas. Long a favourite of designers and design publications on the hunt for something original, Guild has a proven (and well-published) track record for finding appealing objects and talent. As you look through the assortment of beautifully printed wallpapers, colourful woven and embroidered linens, hand-made ceramics, glassware and accessories, you may very well find yourself swearing off mass-produced and flat-packed furnishings for good.

The British love of gardens and 'natural' landscapes is evident in squares and parks around the capital, but a more delicate and unusual green space is a botanical garden that has been a home to specimen and medicinal plants since 1673, when it was planted as the Apothecarie's Garden for educating apprentices in the identification of plants. The riverside setting was chosen for its milder climate, which would support non-native species, and the first greenhouse in England was built here in 1681. A botanist's delight, the highly unusual and varied garden contains over 5,000 taxa and a rich history – cotton seed sent from this garden in 1732 to James Oglethorpe in Georgia helped to establish the crop in the southern colonies. Though away from tourist attractions, the Physic Garden is well worth a detour, especially when it is combined with a walk along the Chelsea Embankment or a look at the nearby Chelsea Royal Hospital, designed by Sir Christopher Wren in 1692.

HIGH-STYLE PUB-RESTAURANT

13 The Enterprise Bar and Restaurant

35 Walton Street

The Enterprise looks like a pub from the outside, but it's
more of a dining room, and a well-loved one at that. Once
an old-fashioned pub it was transformed by hotel-design
duo Tim and Kit Kemp (see also p. 116) into a stylish
restaurant with Kit Kemp's trademark smart, traditional
English furnishings. The Kemps no longer own it, but
still there are creaseless table linens and pale green
upholstery, carved wood details and crisp curtains. The
menu is also high-quality, well-rounded modern European
– Mediterranean-style fish and pasta, grilled rib-eye steak
with Béarnaise sauce and frites; starters of pea soup with
mint and Orkney crabmeat with gazpacho dressing. Being
in such a fashionable area, one wouldn't expect a
dilapidated old boozer, but the Enterprise exceeds anything
you might think lies behind a pub window.

FANTASY WEDDING WEAR

14 Basia Zarzycka

52 Sloane Square

Bursting with sprays and bunches of flowers, this shop
might easily be taken for some kind of fantastical florist's
boutique – and must be seen to be believed. The flowers,
whether sik, ceramic or jewel-encrusted, are all in the
sevice of the fantasy-inspired designs of Basia Zarzycka,
however, as she specializes in elaborate weddings and
evening wear. Everything she touches, from shoes and
bags to wraps, dresses and head-wear, positively blossoms
with colour: straw hats with sprigs of rosemary and sweet
pea, a bag made of pistachio-coloured feathers and
sprinkled with diamante, pink tulle dresses with flowers
'trapped' between the layers, a choker of violet pansies,
floral tapestry shoes. To crown your ensemble, Zarzycka
has a collection of more than 600 tiaras. She also provides
a personal consultation for wedding wear, which includes
making a toile for every bride.

HAND-CRAFTED AND SIMPLE
15 Egg
36 Kinnerton Street

Clothing designers Maureen Doherty and Asha Sarabhai create pieces that can be worn by young and old in relaxed styles that are luxuriously well-made in India using traditional weaving and stitching techniques. From the designs based on traditional work garments to those inspired by 17th-century Indian menswear, the all-natural clothes are easy to wear and practical. Alongside the clothing are exhibitions of largely British contemporary craftspeople; works in ceramic or metal are all 'useful and usable'. The shop in a former dairy, hence the name, is a beautifully kept paean to simple, quality craft, with objects hung or set alongside bright tiles or cool painted walls.

FASHIONABLE SCENE
16 Blue Bar
150

BEAUTY IN THE DETAILS
17 V. V. Rouleaux
54 Sloane Square

'A paradise of *passementerie*' is how Annabel Lewis describes her breathtaking assortment of fine ribbons, bows, tassels and beads. Lewis started out as a florist before she closed up shop in 1990 and began sourcing ribbons from all over the world. Now V. V. Rouleaux is a single-stop destination for trimmings for clothes, furnishings – just about anything that could do with a flourish or a touch of colour or sparkle. With spool upon spool of eye-catching crepe, organdy and silk ribbons – not to mention the flowers, braids and countless other irresistible ornaments, all as appealing as wrapped candy – designers find her emporium invaluable.

PRINCE OF SILVER
18 David Mellor
173

C3a RED CHECK PJS

C7b STRIPED PJS

C7a LAWN PJS

Designer Tracey Boyd has lit up the catwalks with her bright, slim-fitting clothes that range from feminine prints to textured linen to jeans and corduroy. Boyd's own-label shop presents a cool, fashion-conscious face to Elizabeth Street, home to several high-ranking boutiques and cafés. This is the definitive source for Boyd's increasingly popular vintage-inspired line, which has attracted Liv Tyler and Kate Winslet, among others.

A short row of boutiques just off the well-traversed Sloane Street, Pont Street features an intense cluster of indigenous creative design talent. With work for other fashion designers, including Zandra Rhodes, under her belt, Elspeth Gibson opened her boutique here in 1998 to wide acclaim. The appointment-only shop allows Gibson to concentrate on her desirable wispy romantic pieces. Soft focus is achieved by hand-dyeing the fabrics. Hemlines can be highish, and many of the fabrics diaphanously sheer. She has recently introduced a less expensive line, 'Gibson Girl' and a line of luxury bath products. Liza Bruce could be confused with her near neighbour were it not for her uniquely decorated shop, which has had its own feature in *World of Interiors*. Made famous by her custom swimwear, her taste in dress is for the loose and unstructured. The shop also carries modern furniture designed by her husband, Nicholas Alis Vega. Rachel Riley has taken traditional-style children's clothes and sweetly refined them with hand tailoring and beautiful, high-quality fabrics worked in her atelier in France. The results are a nod to the 1950s in crisp cottons and linens, bright polka dots, stripes and custom prints. The finery is not limited to children as Riley makes clothes for women as well.

Her handbags have animated the pages of *Vogue*, *Cosmopolitan* and *Elle*, they've adorned the arms of Madonna, Björk and Elizabeth Hurley. But Lulu Guinness is no slave to fashion: she makes fashion all her own. Call them whimsical, naïve or cartoonish, but her floral prints, 'house' design or signature 'flowerpot' bags are instantly recognizable. Colourful, bright and delightful, her shop has irresistible sweetshop appeal. If her designs remind you of 1950s Parisian fashion plates, that's just one example of old-style glamour that inspires Guinness. Whether it's in wool, satin, velvet or silk, you probably won't find anything like a Guinness bag anywhere else.

The sultry screen idol Gina Lollobrigida was the inspiration for this sexy line of footwear that began in the 1950s. Now owned by three brothers, who took over from their film-fan father, the shop still sells shoes made in East London, and the designs are still slinky, feminine, popular with the fashion-minded and continue to express a certain kind of female glamour. Both the patent 'Phoebe' shoe with four-inch heels and the minimal straps and the flat 'Cleopatra' sandal in white, turquoise or black kid come with the added sparkle of 'crystal diamante'. Ankle boots with painted butterfly patterns, kid leather or stonewashed fabric feature distinctive buckles, and a tall sandal might be topped with suede fringe at the ankle.

GALLERY AND GREENERY

27 Hyde Park
Serpentine Gallery

The largest of the royal parks, Hyde Park's vast green space in the centre of the city contains pockets that each have their particular beauty: from the classic English Rose Garden and romantic 19th-century statuary and an Italianate folly to the Princess Diana Memorial park, one of London's most imaginative play areas, and Speaker's Corner, a magnet for public soapbox-style debate since 1855. Occupying a former tea house is the Serpentine Gallery, which presents world-class contemporary art exhibitions in a more relaxed setting than the severity of so many of the city's galleries and museums. Every summer an internationally renowned contemporary architect is invited to create a folly for the lawns in front of the museum; recent years have seen works by Zaha Hadid, Daniel Libeskind and Toyo Ito (shown above).

SCENTS OF DIFFERENCE

28 Jo Malone
150 Sloane Street

Jo Malone has always believed in personalized skin care, from her days, not so long ago, as a London facialist with 'a handful of devotees'. Her minimalist black and white labels are now recognized and prized in and beyond Britain, but her products are still designed for the needs of the individual. Cleansers and moisturisers designed for daily regimes can be boosted with oils from her specialist range. Malone encourages 'fragrance combining', so all of her 15 original fragrances – for instance, Amber and Lavender, Nutmeg and Ginger, Grapefruit, Verbenas of Provence, Lime Basil and Mandarin – can be layered with others to create an entirely personal scent that can be tested in the shop's fragrance booths. Her recent foray into room scents ('Scent Surround') means you can add the luxury of Jo Malone fragrances to your home or workspace.

Mayfair
Soho
Covent Garden

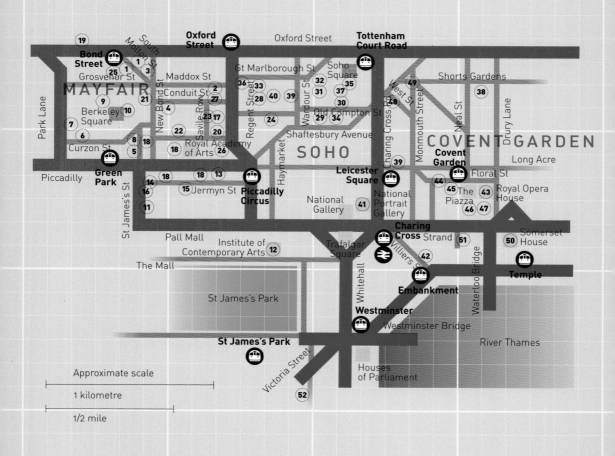

Oxford Street

Oxford Street

Tottenham Court Road

MAYFAIR

Grosvenor St

South Molton St

Maddox St

Conduit St

Gt Marlborough St

Soho Square

Bond Street

Park Lane

Berkeley Square

New Bond St

Savile Row

Regent Street

Wardour St

Old Compton St

Shaftesbury Avenue

SOHO

West St

Charing Cross Rd

Monmouth Street

Shorts Gardens

Neal St

Drury Lane

COVENT GARDEN

Curzon St

Royal Academy of Arts

Covent Garden

Long Acre

Piccadilly

Green Park

St James's St

Jermyn Street

Piccadilly Circus

Haymarket

Leicester Square

Floral St

The Piazza

Royal Opera House

National Gallery

National Portrait Gallery

Pall Mall

Institute of Contemporary Arts

Trafalgar Square

Charing Cross Strand

Somerset House

The Mall

Villiers St

Whitehall

Embankment

Waterloo Bridge

Temple

St James's Park

Westminster

Westminster Bridge

River Thames

St James's Park

Victoria Street

Houses of Parliament

Approximate scale

1 kilometre

1/2 mile

Inevitably and somewhat inexplicably, many visitors to London make their way to Leicester Square, Piccadilly, Regent Street, Covent Garden Piazza. Each in their own way, these places represent for many people London's energy, its metropolitan air, its buzz. Stripped of their local colour, overilluminated by neon, overpopulated by unthinking tourists and often infiltrated by gaudiness, many parts are now little more than symbols of former greatness, their grandeur denuded by the globalizing monoculture. Get quickly away from these magnets and you are in the heart of the West End – dense, chic, lively and ever-changing.

West of John Nash's wonderfully grand Regency boulevard, Regent Street, is Mayfair's dense concentration of high style and fashion, art and commerce. Bisected by Bond Street – lined with a mixture of international fashion labels and classic old shops and galleries – Mayfair is true-blue upmarket London, a genuine oasis of gentility between Piccadilly and Oxford Street. Many of the shops, auction houses and galleries – and therefore also the restaurants and bars – cater to a small group of the wealthy and well-heeled, but there are pockets of affordability for all of us. If you've allowed for a one-off extravagance, this is the place.

Crossing Regent Street going east, you are unmistakably in Soho, flashy and seedy, creative and degenerate, hip and outmoded. The first sign is the once-cool-now-downmarket Carnaby Street, a resonant reminder of how changes in fashion are accelerated in the city centre (though running parallel one street away, Newburgh Street [p. 51] is alive and well). Athough the area's high density of media and creatives maintain Soho's buzz during the day, and recent pedestrianization has made it a generally pleasant place to stroll, its primacy as London's liveliest night spot is slipping eastwards, toward Hoxton Square and Shoreditch. Soho is certainly alive and well and retains its low-key seediness, but there are treasures easily overlooked in the melee that are well worth the hunt.

Since its gentrification in the 1970s, when its old vegetable market was moved to south London, Covent Garden has attracted a largely youthful crowd drawn to the bars and many designer boutiques selling the latest streetwear. With the recent refurbishment and expansion of the Royal Opera House, however, an older, more culturally inclined group demanding higher standards of food and drink has had an impact. The Palladian-style Piazza, designed by Inigo Jones in 1635, is the quarter's centrepiece and tourist mecca, but the small streets and alleyways that surround it have much to offer – if you know where to look.

There are many places to buy designer wear in London, but few have the cachet that Browns has achieved over the past three decades. Joan Burstein and husband, Sidney, opened the shop in 1970, and since then it has become a revered name in London fashion. Browns features well-known designers from all over the world, while Browns Focus, across the street, demonstrates Burstein's prescient eye for young innovators, which is evidenced in the shop's 2001 redesign by one of Britain's most in-demand architects, David Adjaye. Fake London, Frost French, Hussein Chayalan and Maharishi are just a few of the talents showcased in his 'white and black' themed rooms.

In a quiet courtyard between Brook and Bond Streets, an oasis from the retail frenzy a block away, Hush is a lounge bar and restaurant set in a Georgian townhouse. The décor is minimal with flair. Low, boxy seating in the lounge, which also has an enclosed 'boudoir' space for intimate conversation, is strewn with cushions in deep, natural shades. Highly designed, it seeks to offer a 'lifestyle' rather than just a meal, drink or coffee.

While men's grooming habits and styles have wavered over the past century, Trumper's commitment to professional service, for which they have been awarded six royal warrants, has not. Still occupying beautiful period premises, the shop that began catering to London gentlemen in 1875 offers a range of services, from haircuts to facial cleanses to chiropody. They even conduct a 'shaving school' where you can learn the best technique to use at home. Trumper's own range of toiletries are on gleaming display in front, while the full menu of treatments, including the ever-popular wet shave with open razor, are performed at the back of the shop by the waistcoat-wearing professionals.

Michael Faraday was one of the most famous scientists of his time, conducting groundbreaking research and staging public displays of his discoveries, and was widely admired by peers and the public. His inventions, including the electric motor, transformer and generator, have shaped modern life. It was at the Royal Institution, where he started in 1813 and remained until the end of his life, that Faraday made his hugely significant discoveries. Today the institution houses a tribute to his contribution in the form of a reconstruction of his lab and a collection of such items as his original devices for electro-magnetic rotation and induction, the principles behind all current electricity-generating power stations, as well as a fascinating array of other scientific and personal instruments.

9   Mount Street Gardens
Off Mount Street, W1

This wonderfully secret, enclosed green space laid out as a public park in the late 19th century is surrounded by grand Queen Anne–style houses and shaded by giant plane trees. Small, discreet wrought-iron-gated entrances near Carlos Place mean the gardens are usually a peaceful, unpopulated place to sit on a wooden bench. In the southeast corner is the Church of the Immaculate Conception, known as the Farm Street Church, built in 1849 for English Jesuits and containing a high altar by Pugin, architect of the Houses of Parliament.

OLD AND RELIABLE

10   The Guinea
30 Bruton Place

Bruton Place is a quaint little mews off moneyed Berkeley Square, and the Guinea, tucked away down the mews, is a reminder of days past, before the looming buildings surrounding the square were built. The pub, dating back to the 15th century, has a modern restaurant addition that is famous for its classic grills. The small, dark, atmospheric bar is loved by high-flying locals and lucky wanderers alike for its Young's brews and its award-winning steak-and-kidney pies and fine cuts of beef. If the glittering modernity of Mayfair becomes too much, the Guinea is a welcome old-world refuge from the haute cuisine and couture but not from high standards.

THE LATEST FROM HAVANA

11   J.J. Fox & Robert Lewis
19 St James's Street

The joining of J.J. Fox and Robert Lewis represents the marriage of two historic tobacco houses. Christopher Lewis set up his shop in 1787, and the first Havana cigars imported to England were sold by his company, Robert Lewis in 1830. James John Fox began his career as a tobacco trader in Dublin in the 1870s. His company still holds a royal warrant, and in 1997 launched its first own brand of cigars using hand-rolled 100% pure tobacco from Valdrych in the Dominican Republic. In addition to being able to sit in Winston Churchill's favourite chair and have a smoke, aficionados can visit the Fox Museum, located on the shop's ground floor, and trawl through two centuries of cigar memorabilia.

CELEBRATING THE AVANT-GARDE

12   Institute of Contemporary Arts
The Mall

On the grand route that is The Mall, one of London's few processional avenues, the ICA sits discreetly almost hidden beneath the canopy of chestnut trees that line the way. Here in the genteel surroundings of Nash House, built by John Nash in a clean, neo-Classical style in the 1830s, are some of London's most progressive artistic happenings. Exhibitions, talks and performances take place addressing the newest movements and innovators in the art world. The ICA is also a premier venue for global cinema, as well as hosting DJ-piloted 'club nights'. The ICA bar is a groovy drinking spot that stays open until 1 am.

ICE-CREAM DELIGHTS

13   The Fountain Restaurant
Fortnum & Mason, 181 Piccadilly

Messrs Fortnum and Mason opened their grocer's shop on Piccadilly in 1707 and it has been catering to the well-heeled of London ever since. Their food hampers are legendary, providing comfortingly familiar luxuries assembled and ready for eating in the park, in the air or on a train or for delivery around the world. Perhaps the store's greatest treasure is an ice-cream sundae served in the Fountain Restaurant overlooking Jermyn Street. This might seem a rather grand setting for such a childhood treat, especially in a place where caviar and a half bottle of champagne are popular menu items. But anyone who has had the creamy enjoyment of a 'Lazy Sunday Afternoon' or a 'Piccadilly Poppet' will tell you it's not hard to bear the extravagance.

STREET FOR SHIRTS

14   Jermyn Street
169

SUPERLATIVE MEN'S FOOTWEAR

15   John Lobb
162

NEW YORK STYLE, LONDON TWIST

16   The Avenue
135

MAGHREB MAGNIFICENCE

17   Momo
132

Of the several arcades built during the early 19th century, the most famous and longest is the Burlington Arcade (1819). Today, some 70 high-quality shops, many of which are independent, offer a range of clothes, leather goods and jewelry. The smaller Royal Arcade includes a Martí Guixi–designed Camper store, while Princes and Piccadilly Arcades features largely menswear and apparel.

The French-born designer made her name in London in the 1980s, and today her flagship store has expanded to include menswear, home furnishings and a café. Her softly shaped and subtly hued clothing, often in linen, leather, wool blends and chiffon, and her signature knits are remarkable for their relaxed sophistication. While Bond Street is awash with international-label shops, it is relatively devoid of good places to eat, so her café serving Mediterranean-style dishes and gourmet sandwiches is a find.

This left-hander's paradise originally started business in 1968 catering to lefties the world over as a shop in Beak Street and through mail order. For the past 15 years, the diminutive premises on Brewer Street has been owned and run by lefty husband-and-wife team Lauren and Keith Milsom. They stock an extensive range of left-handed products, from their universally acclaimed pair of left-handed scissors to garden tools, kitchen implements and clocks and watches that move anti-clockwise – a collection of more than 200 objects. This is a wonderfully quirky but priceless source for practical items and gifts, and most of their innovative and useful accessories can be tested in the store.

It began as a small bookshop in York, England, in 1761, and more than two centuries later it is internationally renowned, the oldest trading antiquarian bookshop in Britain and possibly the world. Charles Dickens was once a regular customer, as were Siegfried Sassoon and J. P. Morgan. Among the priceless treasures that have lined Sotheran's shelves are a first edition of Shakespeare's *Venus and Adonis* (1599), which was discovered in the attic in 1867. Clients and passers-by are encouraged to come in and browse among their vast selection of volumes.

SPRINGBANK MILLENNIUM SET
25yr 30yr 35y 40yr 45yr 50yr
£ 3500·00

The subdued, neutral tones belie the name, but Circus, at the western edge of Soho, has star appeal. Designed by refined minimalist David Chipperfield, it began as an ultra-hip eatery but has settled into a solid, well-liked restaurant with an elegant lower-level bar and Japanese-inspired garden with enough style and formality to justify its longevity. Starters of beef carpaccio or roasted quail, mains of tuna with soy and cucumber or red mullet with black olives and crushed new potatoes demonstrate the variety on offer.

The worn blue awning of the Vintage House shields a veritable *Wunderkammer* of malt whisky, worth a pilgrimage for the connoisseur. On rows of boxed shelves bottles and bottles of wines, other liquors and cigars share space with sought-after whiskies. Malts from every region and age include special bottlings and collector's decanters. If the thought of lugging a bottle back on the plane seems too risky, you'll just have to drink it before you leave.

A maze of small, mostly pedestrianized streets running behind Regent Street and south of Oxford Street holds everything from chain boutiques to street-market chic. Parallel to the faded funkiness of Carnaby Street is Newburgh Street, a focal point for leading-edge street-fashion boutiques, such as Sharp Eye, Burro (p. 54), and Carhartt, which continually reinvent streetwear for the urban-savvy. The Dispensary sells a range of street-style designer labels; across the street is Jess James, featuring jewelry by young makers. Cinch is a showcase for Levi's Red, a line developed in Brussels and not easy to find elsewhere, with high-tech-looking premises by Dutch design collective Droog.

This small, unpublike bar is a Soho standby. Though it serves beer only by the half-pint, encouraging the consumption of wine instead, it is often too crowded to move your elbows in the late-week evenings and amicably full the rest of the time. Legend has it that this was a hangout of London members of the French resistance and, sitting as it does, surrounded by traditional old pubs and trendy new cafés, it retains the aura of stubborn pride, much like its home country. Delightfully shabby, it has more character in one scratched wine glass than most of the new places put together. The upstairs restaurant is intimate and funky but the food varies with the chef.

THE ART OF CRAFT
36 Liberty
214–220 Regent Street

Arthur Liberty opened his shop on Regent Street in 1875 selling Oriental home ornaments and fabrics, and his mock-Tudor building soon became one of the most fashionable shops in London, drawing such artistically inclined clients as pre-Raphaelites Edward Burne Jones and Dante Rossetti. The store has a long association with crafts (they still have a partnership with Moorcroft), employing Arts and Crafts and Art Nouveau designers to create pieces that are still famously 'Liberty' in style. Despite the contemporary collections and a recent renovation and refit that has significantly updated the store's look and wares, it continues to promote singular, occasionally old-fashioned but wonderfully crafted goods. The ground floor of the Tudor Shop (built in 1924) houses the sumptuous haven of the 'Scarf Hall', where you can find Liberty designs, such as the ostrich-feather pattern, as well as pieces by well-known designers and up-and-coming talents. The lower ground floor is home to Liberty's signature array of crafts pieces and the rather groovy, recently opened Arthur's café.

JAZZ MECCA
37 Ronnie Scott's
47 Frith Street

There are many jazz venues in London, but, set in the heart of Soho's lively nightscape, Ronnie Scott's attracts the biggest international talents. Scott, himself a saxophonist, opened his first club in 1959 with his partner, Pete King, and he was recognized by the Queen in 1981 for his 'services to jazz'. Over the years, the club has featured the very best, Zoot Sims, Stan Getz, Ben Webster, Bill Evans, to name a few. Scott's name is synonymous with jazz in London and abroad, as is the much-revered Frith Street venue, which keeps to the well-loved arrangement of small cocktail tables, dim lighting and low murmurs – all in deference to the artistry of the stage.

POETIC LITTLE LUNCHES
38 Poetry Café
22 Betterton Street

There is more poetry to this little café than the parchment-style lampshades with inked verses scrawled across them.

This is the café of the London Poetry Society. By day it's a pleasant but unassuming little café – away from the madding crowd coursing through Covent Garden's nearby pedestrian zones – where light and inexpensive vegetarian lunches are served. There's plenty of coffee and tea, as well as a full bar. At night it becomes the venue for poetry readings, workshops and music. Tuesday nights feature open-mike poetry; on Saturday evenings, it's poetry and jazz.

ENTERTAINING ADULTS

39 Agent Provocateur

166

FASHION AND ART

40 The Pineal Eye
49 Broadwick Street

It's the eye-like structure that some lizards have to detect changes in light. Combining cutting-edge fashion with avant-garde art, this retail version, established by Yuko Yabiku in 1998 responds to new talent in much the same way, changing with every innovation. Changeable as it is, Pineal Eye has been a consistent source for new British and international talents. Exhibitions of fashion and fine art are carried simultaneously with collections handpicked by Yabiku from among the most cutting-edge and newly emerging designers. Together with the artful shop design, the unique selection of work provides an illuminating glimpse into the heart of the edgier London fashion scene.

TEA WITH A VIEW

41 The Portrait Restaurant

148

DRIPPING WITH HISTORY

42 Gordon's Wine Bar

151

43 Amphitheatre Café and Restaurants
Royal Opera House, Covent Garden

The Royal Opera House was extended to an acclaimed
design to enlarge its facilities and to incorporate it into
Covent Garden Piazza in 1999 The centrepiece of
the renovation is a soaring, arched-glass atrium
that provides glittering bar and restaurant spaces
to complement the Royal Opera's internationally
celebrated programme. And some of the restored rooms
in the original 1858 building offer a particularly grand
experience – the Vilar Floral Hall Balconies, which
overlook the restored Hall (traditional English menu)
and the red-carpeted, neo-Classical-style Crush Room
(cold meals). But to those simply passing by, the
Amphitheatre Restaurant, located on the top floor in
a more contemporary, minimalist setting, and the
Café are open to the general public from Monday to
Saturday for light lunches. Seating on the Terrace,
in good weather, affords spectacular views across
Covent Garden Piazza. Ticket-holders can book pre-
performance, interval and post-performance meals in
the various bars as well as the Crush Room and Vilar
Balconies.

OFF OF THE MAIN DRAG
44 Floral Street
- Maharishi, no. 19
- Paul Smith, nos 40–44
- Burro, no. 29
- Nigel Hall, no. 18

Avoid the tourist magnet that has become the Covent
Garden Piazza and head for the cobblestoned,
pedestrianized Floral Street, where stylish boutiques
and funky one-off shops draw insiders and locals. With
its more subdued and sophisticated air, the street is the
destination for shoppers in search of genuine British
goods – Paul Smith's first store is here. Burro is a street-
wise label aimed at being 'clean-lined and understated',
with screen-printed knits and T-shirts, paint-spattered
canvas shoulder bags, all minimal in design and hues.
Maharishi is a popular British label, designed by Hardy
Blechman, with many deviations on camouflage:
combat and cargo trousers, tiger-stripe T-shirts, in a
range of colours that would stand out in the city more
than the jungle. For a newer arrival on the British men's
designer scene try Nigel Hall's plain-spoken, own-label
shop.

FEMININE INDULGENCE
45 The Sanctuary
12 Floral Street

As the name implies, the Sanctuary is an unexpected
respite from the immediate activity of Floral Street and
a world away. London's most famous women's spa is a
shrine to pampering and relaxation. Even the
uninitiated might recognize the atrium pool with its
rope swing and planted vegetation, as it has featured in
numerous photographs and was used by Joan Collins
in that infamous masterpiece *The Stud*. A separate
exercise pool caters to the fitness-oriented, while the
Thai Seating Area encourages nothing more than
chatting or reading while cocooned in a plush
Sanctuary robe. There are whirlpools, saunas and
rooms for facials, massage and aromatherapy, as well
as home cooking in the Palm Restaurant, all devoted to
the art of de-stressing.

EATING HISTORY
46 Rules
134

BIG NAMES, SMALL THEATRE
47 Donmar Warehouse
41 Earlham Street

The intimate Donmar was opened in 1992 as a not-for-
profit production company under the creative
directorship of Sam Mendes, the director of the highly
acclaimed movie *American Beauty*. It has gained
numerous awards for its fine productions involving
leading directors David Leveaux, John Crowley,
Michael Grandage, Sean Matthias, Phyllida Lloyd, and
critically acclaimed actors Brenda Blethyn, Jim
Broadbent, Charles Dance, Colin Firth, Jane Horrocks
and Elizabeth McGovern. The theatre contains a mere
250 seats but has thrilled audiences with such recent
shows as *The Blue Room* (starring Nicole Kidman) and
Electra, which went on to successes on Broadway,
among their repertoire of new plays and reinter-
pretations of theatre standards.

STYLISH MICRO-HOTEL
48 West Street
126

49 Seven Dials

- Coco de Mer, 23 Monmouth St
- Koh Samui, 65 Monmouth St
- aQuaint, 38 Monmouth St
- Neal's Yard Remedies, 15 Neal's Yard
- Boxfresh, 2 Shorts Gardens
- Neal's Yard Dairy, 17 Shorts Gardens
- Magma, 8 Earlham Street

Once the hangout of thieves and impoverished street vendors, Seven Dials and the area around it was developed in 1693 by Thomas Neale, Master of the Mint, and finished around 1710. It didn't become fashionable, however, until centuries later. Since the gentrification of Covent Garden area in the 1970s and 1980s, this small quarter of narrow, cobblestoned streets and restored buildings has become one of London's most distinctive shopping areas, where hip fashion and vintage shops are interspersed with quirky boutiques on the streets radiating from the the circular intersection of seven medieval roads. In the past decade or so, most of these streets have been re-paved in cobblestone and generally smartened up. A short walk along Shorts Gardens takes you to Neal Street, a parade of shops dominated by a number of stores that specialize in weird and wonderful shoes,from trainers and rock-climbing slippers to patent-leather stilettos. Monmouth Street, running north from Seven Dials, and Upper St Martin's Lane, running south, have become glamorous pockets of design-label boutiques. Coco de Mer, the brainchild of Sam Roddick, daughter of Body Shop entrepreneur and fair-trade pioneer, Anita, is much-publicized venture offering high-fashion lingerie and erotica. Continuing along the east side of the street, you can stop in at the Monmouth Coffee House for a cup of freshly-ground dark stuff before heading to Koh Samui, which features a famously well-chosen selection of top labels and newly arrived names with a good stock of British designers. Across the road, recent arrival aQuaint, opened in 2002 by designer Ashley Isham, stocks the entire collections of a smaller number of mainly British designers. Neal's Yard, sandwiched between Monmouth Street and Shorts Gardens, and entered by way of small alleys off those streets, is a centre for organic eating and holistic treatments – Neal's Yard Remedies sells tonics, creams, oils and aromatherapy ingredients all bottled in the distinctive old-style blue glass. Just outside the courtyard is Neal's Yard Dairy, stacked full of gorgeously pungent regional varieties. At the corner of Earlham Street and Seven Dials, Boxfresh offers bright, funky 'urbanwear'. For those in search of the latest and hottest visual books and magazines, Magma is London's leading store for graphics, design and architecture publications, from local rags to obscure imports.

50 Somerset House
The Strand

- Courtauld Galleries
- The Admiralty
- Riverside Terrace

With an ambitious plan of refurbishment that began in 1997, Somerset House, formerly the forbidding offices of the Inland Revenue, is now home to several art galleres, including one of the country's greatest private art collections, a fine restaurant, terrace dining and lively courtyard fountains designed by architects Jeremy Dixon and Edward Jones. On the site of the first Renaissance palace in England, built in 1550 and demolished in 1775, Somerset House is one of England's finest 18th-century buildings. In 1947 Samuel Courtauld's vast personal collection of Western art was given to London University and in 1990 it was moved to spacious premises in Somerset House. World-famous Old Master, Renaissance, Impressionist and Post-Impressionist paintings are displayed over three floors. The Gilbert collection of European gold and silver and the Hermitage Rooms are also open for public viewing. A welcome break from the cultural riches is the funky-clubby Admiralty, a reference to the naval offices that used to be based here, established by innovative restaurateur Oliver Peyton. While the décor is an intriguing mix of traditional British attitudes and ornaments, as designed by architect Andrew Martin and designer Solange Azagury-Partridge (p. 167), the food is regional French Outside, the Riverside Terrace has been opened for the first time in over 100 years, and you can enjoy a drink or a meal in a magnificent position beneath umbrellas overlooking the Thames. In winter, with a nod to Rockefeller Center in Manhattan, the courtyard is taken over by an outdoor ice rink.

51 Adam Street
142

52 Cinnamon Club
139

1486 M

Marylebone
Fitzrovia
Bloomsbury
Holborn

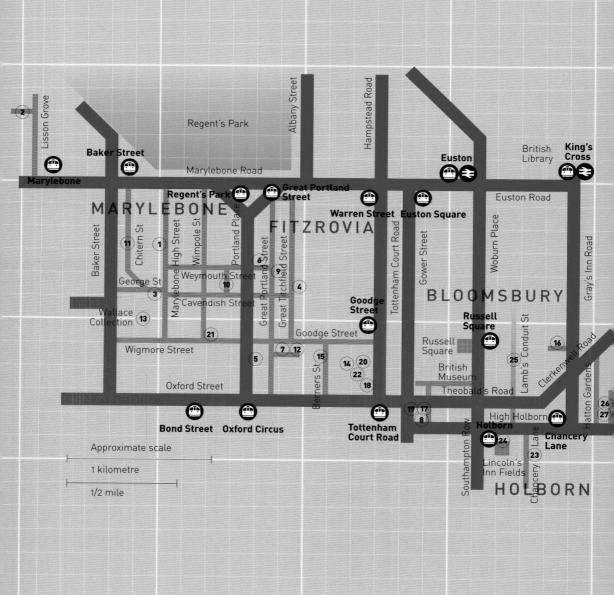

2 Lisson Grove

Regent's Park

Albany Street

Hampstead Road

British Library

King's Cross

Baker Street

Marylebone Road

Euston

Marylebone

Regent's Park

Great Portland Street

MARYLEBONE

FITZROVIA

Warren Street

Euston Square

Euston Road

Baker Street

Chiltern St

Marylebone High Street

Wimpole St

Portland Place

Great Portland Street

Great Titchfield Street

Tottenham Court Road

Gower Street

Woburn Place

Gray's Inn Road

11

1

6

9

BLOOMSBURY

George St

Weymouth Street

10

4

3

Cavendish Street

Goodge Street

Russell Square

Wallace Collection

13

21

Goodge Street

Russell Square

Lamb's Conduit St

16

Clerkenwell Road

Wigmore Street

5

7 **12**

15

British Museum

25

Hatton Gardens

Oxford Street

14 **20**

22

18

Theobald's Road

26

27

Berners St

19 **17**

8

High Holborn

Bond Street

Oxford Circus

Tottenham Court Road

Southampton Row

Holborn

Chancery Lane

Chancery Lane

24

23

Approximate scale

Lincoln's Inn Fields

HOLBORN

1 kilometre

1/2 mile

Marylebone, the area defined roughly by Oxford Street in the south and the Euston and Marylebone Road in the north, is a curious mixture of Edwardian proportions, commercial enterprise, apartment living and discreet stylishness. At the western edge is Marylebone High Street, which, somewhat to the dismay of its loyal inhabitants, has in recent years become one of London's premier gastronomic destinations, with a supporting cast of high-quality shops and design stores. Not far in distance but worlds away from nearby Madame Tussaud's is Chiltern Street, a little-known street with a quirky collection of fine shops. Farther north, past Marylebone Road, is Church Street and Alfie's antiques market, home to a host of antiques dealers well off the beaten track.

Fitzrovia, to the east, is a maze of small and one-way streets inhabited by advertising agencies (like M C Saatchi), engineers (Ove Arup, Buro Happold) and furniture showrooms, making it a hotbed of high design. It gets its name from lovely Fitzroy Square, designed on two sides by the neo-Classicist Adam brothers in the 1790s. The quarter also has older creative associations, but more of the starving-artist sort. Atmospheric pubs that were once the haunts of humble writers (T.S. Eliot drank at the Fitzroy Tavern, for example) and artists retain their shabby chic, while others have cleaned house entirely, in favour of cutting-edge media houses and restaurants with seductive interiors by top designers that give nighttime pursuits an infusion of glamour.

Moving east again, on the other side of Tottenham Court Road, the London moderns take hold in the form of the Bloomsbury set, who made this area the centre of literary modernism. Home to University College, the British Museum and, until the late 1990s, the British Library (now in a Scandinavian-inspired building on Euston Road), Bloomsbury retains the aura of a literary and academic enclave, despite the tourist buses that wend their way through the narrow streets. Pleasing squares provide refuge for and reminders of the area's continuing intellectual pursuits.

John Milton, Francis Bacon and Charles Dickens, as well as Dickens's character Pip — all lived for a time in the place known as Holborn, a somewhat transitional area between the old London of the City and the later developments west. The Inns of Court are located here, with their fine buildings and lush enclosed green spaces, as is the former journalists' mecca, Fleet Street, and the wide avenue of the Strand. The best of Holborn is in the isolated historic gems — London's oldest Catholic church and its neighbouring tavern, an eccentric architect's historic house-museum and the underground vaults now used by dealers in silver.

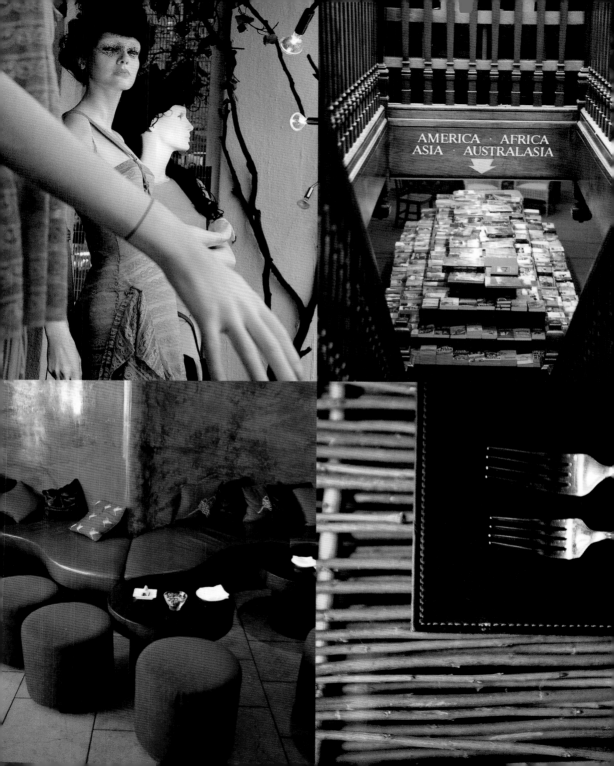

A WORLD OF TRAVEL BOOKS

1 Daunt Books

83–84 Marylebone High Street

Marylebone High Street has a surprisingly pleasant village atmosphere, but Daunt Books would be enough to lure travellers here even without the surrounding shops and cafés. With its Edwardian rooms, there are many who consider it London's most beautiful bookshop. Though a newly opened area is devoted to fiction and children's books, its *pièce de résistance* in both character and design is its foreign section, where James Daunt features not only guides and maps, but histories, fiction and cookery titles – all helpfully arranged by country. The travel section is housed in the beautiful atrium space complete with a gallery running along both walls.

ART DÉCO EXTRAORDINAIRE

2 Gallery 1930/Susie Cooper Ceramics

174

LEBANESE IN COLOUR

3 Fairuz

3 Blandford Street

Named after a singer, whose likeness has been immortalized in oil paintings on the walls, this bright yellow spot of Lebanese cuisine is upbeat, with a fresh menu that critics and diners rave about, a difficult feat in restaurant-rich Marylebone. Popular favourites – tabouleh, falafel and grills – are rounded out with more interesting Lebanese dishes, such as smoked cod roe with garlic and chicken wings, and topped up by complimentary fruit and baklava with coffee.

OF HEARTH AND HOME

4 CVO Firevault

36 Great Titchfield Street

Located in an area swimming with modern- and contract-furniture showrooms, CVO Firevault is an interior décor store with a difference. Taking its name from the elegant hearth designs that can be purchased there, it features an attractive array of objects, clothing (much of it in pale-coloured silk or cashmere) and soft furnishings to enjoy around the glowing flames. The real draw, however, is the downstairs café-bar, whose rich ambiance cannot be divined from the exterior and has made it an atmospheric hideaway.

OPULENT MEZE

5 Ozer

4–5 Langham Place

Langham Place is northern continuation of Regent Street, which features a number of chain-food outlets and one plush, ruby-red pocket that is Ozer, a nouvelle Turkish-Mediterranean restaurant that wins rave reviews for its lush interior and its innovative approach to traditional Turkish cuisine. Chef Huseyin Ozer offers the conventional mixed meze dish as a delectable *belle présentation*, a popular favourite of lunching BBC executives who work up the street. A world away from the very English environment outside, Ozer offers a striking interior, varied menu and service bound by Ozer's personal guarantee of satisfaction.

PEERS OF ARCHITECTURE

6 Royal Institute of British Architects

66 Portland Place

The Royal Institute of British Architects is housed in a grand 1930s building that includes galleries, meeting rooms, a café and a world-class architecture bookshop. With 30,000 members, it is one of the most influential architecture bodies in the world. Regular exhibitions, lectures and events highlight new architecture from around the globe. The contemporary first-floor café, recently remodelled by the Conran group, buzzes with figures from the architecture community and nearby embassies and consulates lining Portland Place.

SUPERIOR MIXES

7 The Social

157

FLORAL FLAIR

8 Joie

10 Museum Street

Just down the street from the British Museum, in an unlikely spot next to an ancient greasy spoon and around the corner from hip dance club The End is Joie, which sells its own line of delicate, diaphanous designs. Its one-off collections have long appealed, in a quiet way, to a discerning fashion crowd, who perhaps catch a glimpse of the collection before hitting the dance floor. The small shop, seemingly overgrown by forest vegetation, is a suitable background to dresses, skirts and tops that are playful and contemporary.

9 Villandry
170 Great Portland Street

Despite their distinctly French affiliations, which includes produce delivered from Paris, the delicatessen and restaurant at Villandry have become something of a Fitzrovia institution. The food shop is a mainstay of many in search of gourmet ingredients, and the dining room boasts rustic French recipes executed with authentic rigour. Should you find yourself in Regent's Park or near Oxford Street, it is a perfect place for a daytime drink or coffee or a light lunch featuring above-par sandwiches of freshly baked bread or nicely accented dishes like pan-fried cod and a great wine list.

PUBLIC HOUSE PLEASANTRIES

10 Dover Castle
43 Weymouth Mews

This Georgian pub, tucked down a mews in a quarter of mainly private and ambassadorial residences – and just a stone's throw from the RIBA headquarters – is the perfect place to settle in for a pint. Whether you choose to admire the 1777 interior and wood-panelled dining room, or to join those who spill out into the mews, you will be among those who live and work here, in a setting visited by few others.

INSTRUMENTS OF PLEASURE

11 Chiltern Street
- Bare, no. 8
- Howarth Woodwind Specialists, nos 31–35
- Philip Somerville, no. 38

Running one street parallel to somewhat nondescript Baker Street (south of the station), Chiltern Street is a delightful row of quirky shopfronts below Dorset Street with a curious orientation toward two distinct groups: brides-to-be and musicians, many of whom come from the Royal Academy of Music near by. The latest boutique to make the street a destination is Bare, a design boutique opened in 2002 by Daisy Morrison and Tina Ferguson. The shop specializes in new talent and distinctly British labels, from cardigans by Pringle and beaded knits by Charlie Wool to tropical-print clutch bags by Nancy Harlem and almost anything by Gharani Strok. For musicians, there are Howarth Woodwind Specialists. Philip Somerville hats add the final touch to the wedding wear available in several of the neighbouring boutiques.

THE ENGLISH SAUSAGE REDUX

12 R. K. Stanley's
6 Little Portland Street

Although the interior of patterned concrete blocks was drawn from the work of Frank Lloyd Wright and diner-style red-leatherette booths may have an American flavour, the fare is distinctly British – sausage, mash and beer. What might seem to be a conventional dish, however, is enhanced by international influences, such as sausages infused with Thai or French seasonings and updated with spicy noodles, chips or gravied mash.

GRAND TOWNHOUSE MUSEUM

13 Wallace Collection
Manchester Square

The often-overlooked Wallace Collection is a privately amassed assembly of art bequeathed to the nation by Lady Wallace, widow of Sir Richard Wallace, in 1897 and opened to the public in 1900. Among the treasures housed in the grand period rooms of this late 18th-century townhouse are a renowned collection of French 18th-century pictures, porcelain and furniture, some fine 17th-century paintings and a rather intriguing armoury. A superb glassed atrium was added in the 2000 renovation and expansion, designed by Rick Mather, providing an ideal place for lunch, tea or a glass of wine.

CLASSIC ENGLISH PIES

14 Newman Arms
23 Rathbone Street

Among the achingly modern restaurants and gastro pubs of London, the Newman Arms, set in a quiet side street just north of Oxford Street, is a small, simple, satisfying locale where the best home-made savoury pies are served. Downstairs is a tight but cosy room for drinks, but the upstairs room with fewer than a dozen tables serves a straightforward menu of pie and puddings – steak and kidney, chicken and broccoli, ham and leek – served with friendliness, little fuss and rather large puff-pastry tops. They serve only lunch, however, and you'll need a good hunger beforehand and a good walk afterwards – especially if you opt for the sticky-toffee pudding for dessert.

IRONICALLY STYLISH ACCOMMODATION

15 The Sanderson
114

16 The Duke (of York)
7 Roger Street

The 1940s are alive and well in this hidden little pub down a narrow street off Gray's Inn Road. You'll certainly need to know it's there, but once you do, you'll be drawn by the warm mustard-yellow walls, the red lacquered piano in the corner, the changing selection of pictures. The back lounge bar is the most captivating, with wood-backed banquettes that give it the feeling of an old railway café or speakeasy. Pubs of genuine interest from periods after the Victorian age are rare in London, so this pre-modern pub has a slightly off-beat ambiance, though the choice of beers and fresh, modern cuisine will appeal to most.

LITERARY LUNCHING
17 Alfred
245 Shaftesbury Ave

Frequently serving the Bloomsbury publishing community and British Museum a few blocks away, Alfred has seen its fair share of literary lunches, but that is not the reason to stop here. Dark purple on the outside, pastel aqua-blue with wood floors and simple formica tables on the inside, Alfred's minimal-traditional interior mirrors its modern British fare in a relaxed manner. Whether you choose the belly pork and red cabbage or scallops in beer batter with black pudding, you'll find updated British cuisine that is interesting but not overly experimental and has resulted in a devoted following among the well-read and not-so-bookish alike.

EASTERN BEAUTY
18 Hakkasan

133

19 James Smith and Son Umbrellas

55 New Oxford Street

The exterior of this shop makes such a wonderful backdrop for photographs that too many people forget to go inside. Yet James Smith and Son really is the ultimate in umbrellas and walking sticks. The first Smith set up shop in 1830 and his son moved the business to these premises in 1857, which has been maintained ever since by the Smith family. With the same fittings specially created for it by its own Victorian craftsmen, this was the first company to make use of the Fox steel frame, which distinguishes the Smith and Son umbrella as the finest in the sky. The company also continues to produce walking sticks, though they may be more at home in the country than the city. Umbrellas range from those created for ceremonial purposes to the everyday, in either solid sombre tones or explosions of vivid colour, and all are working symbols of an era of fine workmanship – and a necessary London accessory.

20 Target Gallery

7 Windmill Street

This unassuming gallery off Goodge Street near Tottenham Court Road has been quietly gaining a reputation for its collection of modernist furniture, ceramics, textiles and glass. The focus is on British makers such as Robin Day, Frank Guille, William Plunkett and John and Sylvia Reid, but there is also a selection of Italian, Scandinavian and French designers, graphics and Pop Art posters, jewelry by Anton Michelsen, Georg Jensen and Hans Hansen, lucite pieces by Lucie Rie for Bimini and a host of other items from the 1930s to the 1970s.

21 Mint

70 Wigmore Street

Mint 'is ethnic, tribal, old and new, solid and pure, handmade ordinary everyday objects presented as extraordinary', according to shopowner Lina Kalafani. This wilfully 'eclectic' range of furnishings, textiles and accessories is arranged over two floors of a former wine store and cellar. Next to an old Tibetan chest you might find a piece by Henry Harris, a pair of felt slippers among the glassware, ceramics and pots.

BRITISH ARTS AND CRAFTS
22 Contemporary Applied Arts
2 Percy Street

Founded in 1948 in the spirit of the turn-of-the-century Arts and Crafts movement, Contemporary Applied Arts is the largest private gallery in Britain for contemporary crafts, with a large regular stock and special exhibitions of all media: fine and costume jewelry, fine metalwork, decorative and functional ceramics, wood, textiles, furniture, glass, bookbinding and paper. Works can be bought on site or commissioned from the hundreds of makers on their books.

SECRETED SILVERWARE
23 London Silver Vaults
53–64 Chancery Lane

The world's largest collection of fine antique silver is housed in 37 shops beneath an unprepossessing building in what were once the strongrooms for the safe deposit of valuables for wealthy Londoners. From 1867, the vaults were guarded night and day, as they are today, and there has never been a robbery. Since 1953, the vaults have been occupied by dealers, and it has been *the* place to find silver, at near dealers' prices. Even if you don't require any Georgian silver plate or Victorian candlesticks, a descent into this quirky arcade is well worth the trip – most Londoners do not even know of its existence.

AN INDOOR FOLLY
24 Sir John Soane's Museum
13 Lincoln's Inn Fields

Sir John Soane (1753–1837) was a distinguished architect (most notably of the Bank of England) and art and artefact collector. During his lifetime he amassed such a huge number of antiquities, archaeological fragments, architectural prints and drawings that, even before he died, his house was known as the 'Academy of Architecture'. The house was completed in 1824, and in 1837 upon his death, Soane bequeathed the house and its contents to trustees with the mandate that it be preserved in its original condition. A visit to the Soane, a jewel-box of delights and surprises with its nooks and crannies and architectural oddities, is a trip into one man's obsessions and love. If that weren't enough, there are paintings by Canaletto, Turner and Joshua Reynolds, two series by Hogarth, Roman marbles and an Egyptian sarcophagus. A particular treat is the first Tuesday of each month, when the museum is open in the evening and the rooms are lit with candles.

RESTORED AND GENTRIFIED
25 Lamb's Conduit Street
• The Perseverance, no. 63
• Cigala, no. 54
• The Lamb, no. 94

The conduit, a recently pedestrianized street, is named for its orginal function as an Elizabethan dam to a tributary of the old Fleet River, which was restored by philanthropist William Lamb in 1577 to bring fresh water to the area. Today, the narrow street is home to an increasing number of stylish restaurants and shops catering to the area's professionals. One of its main attractions is the Lamb, a pub that retains its Victorian interiors, including its 'snob screens', pivoting partitions that hid drinkers from view. The modern-rustic Spanish restaurant and bar Cigala serves critically convincing tapas and larger dishes and an intriguing selection of wines. The Perseverance epitomizes the gastro-pub of today, with a modern make-over, fresh food, cleverly selected wine list and the enduring conviviality of the public house.

SANCTUARY OF AGES
26 St Etheldreda
Ely Place

One of London's most intimate and atmospheric churches, St Etheldreda was built in about 1293 and is the oldest surviving Catholic church the city. In the early 17th century it was a place of refuge for persecuted Catholics. Much of the little church was damaged in the Second World War, not, however, the walls of the undercroft, which contain Roman foundations dating from the third century. The undercroft itself was once used as a tavern, but nowadays visitors have the pleasure of slaking their thirst in the equally diminutive rooms of the Olde Mitre Tavern near by.

ANOINTED PUB
27 Ye Olde Mitre Tavern

152

SIR JOHN SOANE'S
MUSEUM
Open Tuesday-Saturday
10 AM ~ 5 PM
(6-9 pm on the first Tuesday
of the month)

ADMISSION FREE

Groups must book in advance
TEL: 0171-405-2107

Lecture tour on Saturday 2:30

LAMBS CONDUIT
STREET WC1

Clerkenwell
Islington
King's Cross

The areas north of Smithfield – or 'smooth field' as it was once known – Clerkenwell, King's Cross and Islington, amply demonstrate how out of a dense urban fabric new life and vitality can emerge. On the border of the City, acting as a kind of fulcrum between it and its lively northern neighbours, is the church of St Bartholomew the Great, which stands proud amid all the surrounding redevelopment. Smithfield Market, a place for cattle and horse trading since the Middle Ages (today a meat market) signals a modern transition with nightclub-goers herding into the Victorian warehouse buildings turned dance venues.

Conversions continue in Clerkenwell, north, a district once known for its light industrial buildings and lively printing presses, many of which have become stylish lofts. Animated by journalists from *The Guardian* newspaper, members of the youth-style magazine *The Face* and a number of internationally renowned architectural figures, such as Zaha Hadid, Clerkenwell embodies that typical London alchemy in which the old world and new ideas fuse into something exciting and unexpected.

Islington, northward again, is another area of successful regeneration. In the 19th century it was one of London's first suburbs, with some of the most unusual and intimate residential squares. Its central-fringe location made it attractive to artists, writers and City bankers, who poured in during the 1970s to refurbish and restore neglected buildings. Today it is one of the most lively and creative of London's villages and still marked by patrician elegance. And although Upper Street, the neighbourhood's main thoroughfare, is lined by chain stores, street markets, such as Camden Passage (p. 83), independent boutiques and bars ensure the area maintains its street style. Islington is also enlivened by the highest density of theatres in London, making it a popular stomping ground for thespians and theatre mavens.

King's Cross, which was known until very recently as just a train station, is now considered a neighbourhood in its own right. The imminent arrival of the high-speed rail link to Paris (a mere 2.5-hour ride away) has spawned numerous loft developments coinciding with a profusion of groovy bars and shops. Some people have appreciated the neighbourhood's off-beat feel for years: archminimalist John Pawson has his studio here, as do the corporate-branding gurus at Wolff Olins. Even though these areas are just outside the ring of tourist attractions (but within an easy walk of the British Library), they have a strong local character that is enriched by the creative and literary people who live there.

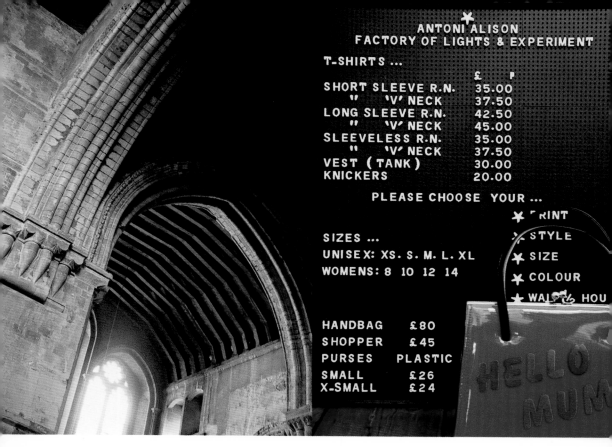

ANTONI ALISON
FACTORY OF LIGHTS & EXPERIMENT

T-SHIRTS ...

	£	P
SHORT SLEEVE R.N.	35.00	
" 'V' NECK	37.50	
LONG SLEEVE R.N.	42.50	
" 'V' NECK	45.00	
SLEEVELESS R.N.	35.00	
" 'V' NECK	37.50	
VEST (TANK)	30.00	
KNICKERS	20.00	

PLEASE CHOOSE YOUR ...

✱ PRINT
✱ STYLE
✱ SIZE
✱ COLOUR
✱ WAIST & HOU

SIZES ...
UNISEX: XS. S. M. L. XL
WOMENS: 8 10 12 14

HANDBAG	£80
SHOPPER	£45
PURSES	PLASTIC
SMALL	£26
X-SMALL	£24

HELLO MUM

CHARMED CHAPEL

1 St Bartholomew the Great

West Smithfield

In a lovely preserved corner of narrow streets lined with traditional-style pubs and shops just across from Smithfield Market lies this small, often overlooked church, the only vestige of the priory founded along with the old St Bartholomew's Hospital (now St Bart's) in 1123 by the Augustinian Rahere. Sections of the church have been rebuilt – the Lady Chapel in 1336, central tower in 1628 – and it fell into disrepair until it was restored in the late 19th century. Today it has an intimate, spare interior, an oasis in a bustling city centre, recently used as the backdrop to the film *Shakespeare in Love,* a little illumination of medieval London.

BOUDOIR-CHIC HOTEL

2 The Rookery

113

'FACTORY OF LIGHTS AND EXPERIMENT'

3 Antoni & Alison

43 Rosebery Avenue

Known for their quirky and wry photographic-print T-shirts and whimsical accessories, Antoni Burakowski and Alison Roberts gained notoriety with their refreshingly humorous catwalk shows. Now their energy and bravado have been channelled into creating a full-blown collection of street-savvy ready-to-wear pieces, including knitwear, dresses, skirts and trousers.

MARKET FRESH

4 Smiths of Smithfield

141

'NOSE TO TAIL DINING'

5 St John

144

Over the past ten or so years, Clerkenwell has become a mecca for young designers of all media and gradually yielded to patches of gentrification. At the heart of the revitalization is Clerkenwell Green, historically a staging ground for the rebellious and disenchanted. Today it is a pleasant Georgian square landmarked by the spire of St James's church, and features shops selling brilliant original creations: C2+ carries a selection of one-off textiles, scarves, neckties, throws and large wall-hangings. The Lesley Craze Gallery has established itself as a showcase for new designs in precious jewelry and carries pieces by over 100 British-based artists. For an antidote to any shopping extravagances, visit the Marx Memorial Library, home to waves of revolutionaries, with a subscription library specializing in socialist literature, which was opened in response to the Nazi book-burnings. The entrance features a 1933 anti-capitalist fresco and small souvenir stand.

A typical pre-club venue for nearby dance clubs (like Fabric, on Smithfield Market), Fluid has developed a following all its own. Suffused with a red glow, it's the kind of bar in which you become immersed. Low sofas provide home comforts, but exoticism is offered in the Japanese undertheme, evidenced in the wide range of sushi and hot food and downstairs club events.

PLAIN AND SIMPLE
9 Quality Chop House

92–94 Farringdon Road

The exterior of the Quality Chop House, around the corner form Exmouth Market in the media-dominated Farringdon Road, looks like it has been around for centuries and that the menu hasn't changed much in that time. In fact, it has been around since the 19th century but in its present incarnation, thankfully for diners at least, for about a dozen years. Though 'progressive working-class caterer' is etched on the front window, and paper napkins, jarred condiments and a plain menu suggest a certain humility, the dishes, as prepared by chef Charles Fontaine, are upwardly mobile and cater to the journalists, bankers, creatives and locals alike. Classic dishes, such as jellied eels and grilled lobster, are served in a classic setting of high-backed settle benches. It's not luxurious, but it is quality.

FUNKY STREET
10 Exmouth Market

- Moro, nos 34–36
- Edible, no. 60
- EC One, no. 41
- Applied Arts Agency, no. 30

This pleasant little semi-pedestrianized parade of boutiques, restaurants and shops has been quietly re-inventing itself over the past ten or so years. On Monday mornings stalls lining the street reflect the area's rising prosperity: woven bags, gourmet sausages, cheeses, olives, oils. While a few old shops remain, a number of spaces have been taken over by trendsetters. Moro caused a spicy sensation when it arrived a few years ago, serving hearty, interesting North African– and Spanish-inspired tapas and main dishes, such as sausages, Portuguese bread salad, garlic prawns and spicy potatoes, all of which go wonderfully with your sangria, cocktails or imported wine. Edible, a food store with a difference, is a relative newcomer that made

culinary headlines with its offerings of chocolate-dipped grasshoppers and other unlikely munchies. The store mainly caters for parties, but their unique selection of edibles can be purchased in the shop. EC One sells 'fashion-led and precious jewelry from over 30 new and established designers'. With a thoroughly innovative collection and shop, and items selling for as little as £40 for a perspex bracelet, as well as a range of bespoke wedding and engagement rings designed by partner and goldsmith Jos Skeates, EC One has quickly become a favorite in the fashion press and with the design-oriented public. The Applied Arts Agency focuses on designers from the UK and Europe working with ceramics, textiles, furniture, wood and metal. Detailed information is available on each piece and some works can be produced on commission.

DANCE ELECTRIC
11 Sadler's Wells
Rosebery Avenue

On the site of a well believed to have medicinal properties, Thomas Sadler built a 'musick' house in 1683 to provide a variety of entertainments for the many visitors looking to take the cure, and there has been some kind of theatre on the site ever since. Today Sadler's Wells is primarily a theatre of modern dance, presenting an international and highly regarded programme. The new building completed in 1998 has a modern appeal and facilities, as well as three bars, café and exhibition area. Recent performances have ranged from a modern retelling of Stravinsky's *Rite of Spring* perfomed by French experimental choreographer Angelin Preljoca, a production of *Madame Butterfly* and a passionate Andalucian version of *Carmen* to the wildly energetic percussion extravaganza *Stomp*.

12 Three Kings
7 Clerkenwell Close

Offsetting the elegance of the Georgian-period St James's Church, papier-mâché lettering and painted figures of this fanciful pub make for a happy contrast. The red and yellow walls are hung with large, brightly coloured puppets that have movable parts, while the bar serves a good range of English and imported lagers and ales. Being right near of the creative hub of the Clerkenwell Workshops (27–31 Clerkenwell Close), this quirky-traditional public house also hosts photography exhibits.

CONTEMPORARY CRAFTS
13 Crafts Council
44A Pentonville Road

Leading up from King's Cross, Pentonville Road is large, noisy and not particularly friendly to the senses, but the Crafts Council, just around the corner from the Angel tube station at the bottom of Islington's Upper Street, is friendly indeed. Britain's largest crafts gallery holds over 1200 works in metal, paper, plastic, ceramic, glass, wood, automata, bookbinding and other media in its permanent collection. Set up as an outlet to make crafts accessible to the public in 1972, it has become a major source of support and promotion for craftsmen and -women around the country. Works on display represent a range of new and established makers, as does the gallery shop where craft pieces can be purchased or commissions arranged. The range of objects is enormous, and a good way for the public to see crafts as a constantly evolving artistic form.

CIVILIZED AFTERNOON
14 The Crown
116 Cloudesley Road

As increasingly ubiquitous gastro-pubs go, the Crown is an old favourite. Established several years ago on a quiet street away from the traffic and in the heart of the Barnsbury conservation area, it can be relied upon for pleasant food and atmosphere, a clever selection of wines, Hoegaarden blond beer and Czech pilser Staaropramen on tap. The clientele is a good mix of locals and youngish newcomers who come from across London to sink into the deep leather sofas with a newspaper on a Saturday or Sunday afternoon and enjoy a quiet pint, while weekend lunchtimes and evenings are buzzing with friends and families. The Mediterranean-tinged menu changes seasonally, but the big chips served with soured cream and chili sauce, salads and Sunday roasts are good standbys.

ORGANIC GOURMET PUB
15 Duke of Cambridge
30 St Peters Street

In the genteel Canonbury neighbourhood of Islington, the Duke of Cambridge signals a welcome parting with tradition. Geetie Singh and Esther Boulton have revamped an old corner pub to create an organic foodie haven – the 'world's first' – with few complaints and a barrage of compliments. In true gastro-pub style, the basic period details of the old place have been preserved brightened up with some paint and a wine list (featuring 50 organic wines), innovative menu and separate dining area. In addition to receiving acclaim for the quality of its food, the Duke bills itself as having received the stamp of the Soil Association for its produce. With sister pub the Pelican (p. 17) in Notting Hill, the Duke serves up such hearty seasonal dishes as pumpkin and rosemary soup, seared pigeon breast and ribeye steak, dishes they describe as 'British rustic with a regional European influence'.

ITALIAN FUTURISTS
16 Estorick Collection
39A Canonbury Square

Eric Estorick was an American writer and sociologist who lived in England after the Second World War and, with his wife, Salome Dessau, started collecting 20th-century Italian art. The couple travelled frequently to Italy and met many of the artists they came to admire. Their lively collection has been featured in museum exhibitions since the 1950s but found its home, in a restored Georgian manor off picturesque Canonbury Square, only in 1998. The collection focuses on Italian Futurist works and figurative art dating from 1890 to the 1950s. Giacomo Balla, Umberto Boccioni, Carlo Carrà, Gino Severini, Luigi Russolo and Ardengo Soffici are all represented, as are Giorgio De Chirico, Amedeo Modigliani, Giorgio Morandi, Mario Sironi and Marino Marini. The lovingly kept small museum also has an art library, café and bookshop.

A small lane lined with Georgian townhouses between Essex Road and Upper Street and filled with intriguing independent shops and boutiques, Cross Street makes a pleasant detour from the crowds. Tribe sells kilims and rugs in bold geometric patterns, mostly from Afghanistan and with a contemporary quality all specially sourced by the owners. Fandango offers unexpected mid-century modern treats like 'Sputnik' hanging lamps and Arne Jacobsen chairs. Suzy Harper has wispy dresses and blouses in quality cotton and linen. With its finely woven scarves, shawls, jackets and other textiles made in India to designs conceived in-house, Canal is a visual and textural delight. No. 40 is the Cross Street Gallery, a small space specializing in contemporary paintings and prints by artists such as Bridget Riley.

Where Upper Street has largely been taken over by large chains, Essex Road running very close by represents the edgier, funkier side of affluent Islington. No longer known for 'fine mansions and ancient inns', its antiques and vintage shops spill north from Camden Passage. Gotham Angels is a bright pink and yellow spot selling its own-label photo-print and bold designs, as well as a number of other young British names. Farther north, Comfort and Joy is a small shopfront with workshop in the back, where retro-style womenswear is churned out carefully, one piece at a time. Historic Essex Road is found in the Old Queen's Head, originally Elizabethan, torn down in 1829 and rebuilt with its original 16th-century plaster ceiling and chimneypiece intact. A quirky favourite is Get Stuffed, a taxidermy shop where you can buy a stuffed lion, wolf, peacock, kangaroo or just about any other animal, as well as the glass case to keep it in.

Upper Street has seen great changes over the past 20 years, culminating recently in a double-level mall full of big-label stores and movie theatres. Despite its over-commercialization, the exceptional aspects that have made Islington a local and international destination – theatres, crafts, antiques, restaurants – are still thriving. Close to Angel at the south end is Camden Passage antiques market, which most agree is London's best antiquarian treasure trove. The King's Head is a pub-cum-theatre that features everything from solo performances to vaudeville and Irish music. Those seeking modern furniture and domestic objects should head for Twenty Twenty-one, while After Noah features reproduction, vintage and contemporary objects presented in an artfully nostalgic mix. For a sense of what the locals buy, head for the family of Gill Wing shops – where stores sell cookery items, shoes, quirky lifestyle accessories and gadgets, menswear and jewelry. The longer-lasting off-shoot of a defunct but once trend-setting restaurant, Euphorium Bakery delights with gourmet bread and pastries. For new Gothic silverworks, Stephen Einhorn has grown from producing skulls and crosses to a whole range of jewelry for men and women. For an appropriate old-new dining experience, try the gastro-pub cooking at The Independence, where the downstairs bar is as laid back as you like but the pale-blue walls ornamented by fleur de lys upstairs signal the transition to fine dining and a menu worth getting hungry for. When the activity and shopping have finally worn you down, head for Highbury Fields in which Upper Street terminates at its northern end. An elegant and broad green ringed by exceptional examples of Georgian houses and dotted with giant trees, it offers space, peace and a bit of nature to offset the bustle behind.

21 Almeida Theatre
Almeida Street

Since it opened as a performance venue in 1980, the Almeida has become one of the most highly regarded small theatres in London. It formed its own producing company in 1990, and in July 2002 Michael Attenborough was named artistic director. The fully refurbished and modernized 1837 building re-opened in mid-2003 with a full programme. The Almeida has long been a favourite not only of the adoring public, but of actors, who don't mind leaving the lights of the West End for tree-lined Islington. Ticket prices tend to be very reasonable, and the venue offers a friendly, intimate theatrical experience.

ANTIQUES EMPIRE
22 Camden Passage Antiques Market
Off Upper Street
• The Mall, 359 Islington High Street
• Lola's, inside The Mall
• Frederick's, 106 Camden Passage
• Annie's, 12 Camden Passage
• Tadema, 10 Charlton Place

Revived from the doldrums in the 1960s, Camden Passage is a hive of antiquarian activity on Wednesdays and Saturdays that is almost hidden from the many shoppers who come to the busy Islington Upper Street. Most of the stalls and shops are secreted behind the buildings on the eastern edge of the main street and within The Mall, which is full of tiny glassed-in spaces selling everything from antique tiaras and tea services to Art Déco ceramics and wooden sailing ships. At The Mall there is a showroom for furniture lighting and clocks downstairs and a restaurant upstairs, Lola's, with an upscale menu that is winning acclaim with chef Hywel Jones, who earned a Michelin star at the much-lauded Foliage just before leaving. Opposite The Mall is Frederick's, an Islington institution featuring a large conservatory and post-hunting luxuries like lobster and beef. A number of Camden Passage shops keep regular hours beyond market days. Annie's vintage clothing, for example, is filled with extravagant beaded flapper dresses and lacey Victorian linens. Tadema has immaculate Art Nouveau, Jugendstil and Arts and Crafts jewelry. A number of specialist antiques shops also line the passage, where tables of a wide range of quality goods come out on the market days. A profusion of glass, silver, bottles, boxes and jewelry fills the cramped rooms of the Pierrepont Row and, farther down, the 'Georgian Village' has three floors of porcelain, silver and jewelry just past the teddy bears and antique dolls at no. 34.

A STEP BACK IN TIME
23 Jerusalem Tavern
55 Britton Street

The small, atmospheric old tavern is named after a local pub once frequented by the likes of Dr Johnson and David Garrick. Housed in a building that dates from 1720, the Jerusalem has preserved its lovely Georgian interiors and intimate snugs and added the attraction of quality beer and ale. It's the only place in London to serve the full range of the Suffolk brew St Peter's, in addition to its popular fruit beers – grapefruit and elderberry – which are offered alternately on tap, along with traditional dark beer, Golden ale and a rotating selecion of other draughts. Two organic beers are also available. Originally a coffee house, the Jerusalem was taken over by John Murphy, of St Peter's, in 1995, and its surprisingly recent incarnation as a pub fits the old place like one of its well-worn wooden settles. A good and reasonably priced menu is also on offer.

COOL COCKTAILS
24 Match Bar
45–47 Clerkenwell Road

This low-key lounge bar is the first of what is becoming a veritable bar-club empire around the city. From its groovy beginnings in Clerkenwell, owner Jonathan Downey, who's on a mission to elevate how and what people drink in London, has gone on to launch Milk & Honey and the Player, both in Soho. Here, the focus is on pleasantly cool rather than hypertrendy, with a large, original drinks list that has introduced beer-swilling locals to the art of the cocktail. A number of places have come and gone in the area, but with its squared-off booths, sunken bar and warm lighting the Match Bar has stood the test of time.

RED-LIGHT ZONE
25 Ruby Lounge
157

WINE IN TRANSIT
26 Smithy's
150

City
Brick Lane
Shoreditch

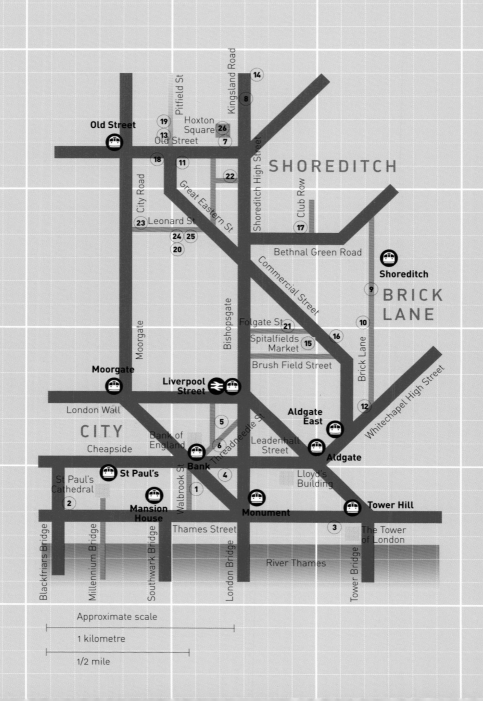

Old London, the Square Mile, the City — all refer to the original settled area on the Thames, the area once ruled by the Romans, now largely known as the financial district, but still imbued with the mystique of the ages. The 11th-century Tower of London was William the Conqueror's declaration of triumph; St Paul's Cathedral a signal of rebirth after the Great Plague of 1665 and the Great Fire of 1666 and a symbol of strength during the Second World War. The City is rife with history and the characters of history — Spenser and Chaucer were born here and Shakespeare flourished here. Nowhere is the fabric of history more tangible than in the architecture — the oldest, smallest, quirkiest streets matched by the public houses that have stood for centuries are set off by the span of bridges and the profusion of early 18th-century churches. Massive rebuilding after the Second World War wasn't particularly design-conscious, but new life has come to the old city, and buildings once threatened with demolition are being saved by the revitalization of marketplaces.

One of the most successful centres of civic rejuvenation is north of the City in the area known as Shoreditch. Once a wasteland of disused light industrial buildings, it has progressed from arty bohemian village to almost upscale status. Artists still occupy many of the loft spaces, as do galleries and design-label boutiques featuring local talent. Its artistic profile is heightened by the presence of the White Cube gallery on Hoxton Square, which has lost much of its edginess but not its edge. If you're looking for innovation in music, art and fashion before it gets to the high street, it probably starts here.

Farther east, amid the cacophony of sights and smells that is the East End, Brick Lane, where the rag trade, Indian restaurants and odd design experiments converge, is attracting its fair share of creatives. This was once a track used as a route for transporting tiles and bricks during the rebuilding of London after the Great Fire. Spitalfields was an early home to nonconformists, later a Jewish ghetto, then, beginning in the 1960s, a community of largely Bangladeshi immigrants. The area was steeped in their culture, and Brick Lane became synonymous with homestyle curry. But change continues, and both the creative industries and the cuisine have experienced injections of new talent and innovation. The Truman Brewery complex has become a centre for fashion, art and design, while young entrepreneurs have elevated the curry house from its humble origins. On the weekends, Brick Lane has a lively atmosphere, with wonderful food and an ever-changing kaleidoscope of one-off boutiques.

CHRISTOPHER WREN CHURCH
1 St Stephen Walbrook
Walbrook Street

There has been a church on this site since before 1096; the previous one, having been built in 1439, burned down in the Great Fire of 1666. Christopher Wren, architect of St Paul's, rebuilt the current St Stephen in 1679 using some methods he would later employ in the great cathedral, including the large central dome, described by one observer as 'a bubble of light'. Although damaged in bombing during the Second World War, it retains its 17th-century features, such as the communion rails, pulpit and font, making for a fascinating glimpse into the mind and career of one of London's greatest architects.

ART NOUVEAU PUB
2 The Blackfriar

153

REFECTORY REVISITED
3 The Vestry
All Hallows by the Tower, Byward Street

Too often a city's greatest sights are surrounded only by woefully touristy places to eat and drink. This is certainly true about the Tower of London, but the recently opened Vestry, at the base of 11th-century All Hallows by the Tower, is a welcome exception. On the site of the old vestry a modern and stylish new eatery with a vaguely monastic air caters both to City big-wigs and savvy travellers. Apart from the pleasing dark woods and plain utensils, the space is airy, well-presented and complements the light menu, which features mussel bisque, stuffed sardines, pork fillet with lemongrass and chili and a tantalizing lavender set cream for dessert.

CROOKED LITTLE PUBLIC HOUSE
4 Jamaica Wine House
12 St Michael's Alley

This, London's first coffee house, reeks with history even after a recent refurbishment has propped up sagging timbers. The first building was damaged in the Great Fire but stood long enough to survive the Cornhill Fire of 1748 and become known for its trade in rum, when it was frequented by 'nothing but aquatic captains'. The Jamaica Wine House was established in 1869, and there it stands, up an old alleyway, beckoning with tamer substances a suited clientele who make their money in banking highrises rather than on the high seas.

CHAMPAGNE AT THE TOP
5 Vertigo[42]

CITY-STYLE LUXURY
6 Threadneedles

BRIT-ART EPICENTRE
7 White Cube
48 Hoxton Square

The light industrial buildings of Shoreditch have been home to artists and galleries since they first became vacant in the slowdown of production decades ago, and some claim that London's East End now has the highest concentration of artists in Europe. White Cube is the offspring of Jay Jopling's Duke Street gallery in Mayfair, a vital catalyst of the Brit Art movement. The new White Cube, on Hoxton Square, has recently added two storeys and become Jopling's headquarters, as well as offering a lot more room – 2000 square feet of open, toplit space under 15-foot ceilings. With a list of artists that includes Damien Hirst, Tracey Emin, Nan Goldin and Lucian Freud, the gallery is a perfect insight into current – if not future – taste in British art.

GRITTY AND HIP
8 Kingsland Road
- Viet Hoa Café, nos 70–72
- Dream Bags Jaguar Shoes, nos 34–36
- Bridge and Tunnel, 4 Calvert Avenue

Hoxton Square has established a firm foothold in Shoreditch nightlife, but Kingsland Road – a couple of blocks away – is the place to experience an edgier emerging scene. Fuelling the groove alongside some of the late-night hangouts like Herbal and Unda da Bridge is the bar Dream Bags Jaguar Shoes, whose vestigial sign as a former import shop belies the hipness created by co-owners Nick and Teresa Letchford. The Bridge and Tunnel bar and dining room – doubtless a reference to the rather pejorative New York expression – comes from the creators of mega-club Fabric (on Smithfield Market), a one-room space and basement with a big state-of the-art sound system. North of the bridge, in little Vietnam, lies Viet Hoa, long a destination for the area's artists, DJs and designers who come to eat their favourite dishes in what many people consider to be the best Vietnamese restaurant in London.

9 Brick Lane

A street long associated with the Asian inhabitants of the area, the concentration of Indian and ethnic restaurants and the lively Sunday market that fills the lane with stalls and bargain-hunters, Brick Lane has most recently become a centre of cutting-edge art and design. Starting from north (above Bethnal Green Road) is Tatty Devine, selling funky jewelry, T-shirts and art from its brick red shopfront. A few doors down (open on Sundays only), Paris-born Olivier Geoffroy has set up his furniture shop, Unto This Last, in a former pub to sell his beautifully formed birch-ply tables: chairs, bookshelves and room accessories that are generated and cut by computer before being assembled. Tiny periwinkle pink Herbal Linea will draw you in with scents of lavender, frankincense and myrrh in its creams, oils and potions. Crossing Bethnal Green you enter the area of Brick Lane proper, where the first indication of the design takeover is Overdose on Design. The shop and workshop of @Work features innovative and uninhibited jewelry designs: for example, silver cherry charm bracelets by Amanda Coleman, photoprinted lucite pieces by Marmalade, chunky stamped silver rings and pendants by Cross Japon.

Passing the Truman Brewery (see next entry) and the art space opposite, you enter a dense realm of Indian and Bangladeshi restaurants. In the past such establishments were synonymous with rooms decorated in dark patterned carpets, flocked wallpaper and garish art all crammed together. Now the trend is for clean, spare design, with modernized ethnic cuisine to match. The bright purple Le Taj sets the new style with white walls, modern furnishings and an innovative menu of Indian and Bangladeshi cuisine. The Preem Balti House is a popular and more traditional favourite.

To cater to the thriving creative community, Brick Lane has also become an epicentre of nocturnal activity. In front of the Truman Brewery office complex is Vibe Bar, whose largely dance-tinged music remains a solid favourite. Across the lane and slightly south an unmarked

door leads to the vast club space that is the Boiler House, a recently converted, unexpectedly huge warehouse that hosts a variety of club nights, exhibitions and a relaxed café. And when the late-night hunger induced by hours of dancing takes hold, revellers from throughout London head for the 24-hour Brick Lane Beigel Bake, which sells bagels baked on the premises and accompaniments (salt beef, smoked salmon, cheese, tuna or herring) to anyone prepared to stand in a queue and shout their order.

ARTISTIC EXPRESSIONS
10 Truman Brewery
91–95 Brick Lane
- Eat My Handbag Bitch, 6 Dray Walk
- Café 1001, 1 Dray Walk
- Junky, 12 Dray Walk

The Truman Brewery complex is identifiable by the bridge over Brick Lane (at about its midpoint) and a small walkway that is today a shoplined pedestrian area. Though only barely marked, Dray Walk is heralded by the bright-orange Café 1001, a good place to stop for a toasted focaccia sandwich, a fruit smoothie or coffee. Wander down the row of shops within the complex, and you'll find exhibition spaces, galleries and a shop or two, such as provocatively titled Eat My Handbag Bitch, which sells an astute selection of mid- and 20th-century furniture classics and design objects. Junky, not your average designer shop, sells 'recycled' clothes: new fashion-designer wear that has been bought as overstock and completely reinvented – a man's suit jacket becomes a women's halter, a pinstriped suit becomes a pair of 'magic trousers' and lovely 'patchwork' skirts. Remix is the spirit of the area.

TRUE ECCENTRIC
11 The Foundry
84–86 Great Eastern Street

This unlikly bar, teetering on the corner of a busy intersection, stubbornly refuses to give in to the wave of gentrification sweeping the area. The Foundry is a resolutely unfinished space where all is high bohemia. Disused televisions and computer monitors suspended from the ceiling or mounted on display; an arrangement of toy dolls hanging near the entrance, silver-wrapped ceiling services, a small van that dispenses hot coffee in the mornings, parked oddly near the DJ's station, and everywhere chipped plaster and paint and worn-out furniture – there is artistic spirit here, supported by its lively and often bizarre programme of performances and exhibitions.

MODERN ART ETC.

12 The Whitechapel Art Gallery
80–82 Whitechapel High Street

With its commitment to show fine works by known and new international and British artists, the Whitechapel Art Gallery is one of London's premier art galleries, housed in a soaring Arts and Crafts building, designed by Charles Harrison Townsend, off the beaten path in a gritty area of London near the southern end of Brick Lane. Established in 1901 to 'bring great art to the people of the East End of London', the Whitechapel names Picasso, Mark Rothko and Jackson Pollock among its early shows. More recently international contemporary artists Nan Goldin, Mark Wallinger and Carl Andre have held exhibitions in the space.

ALL ABOUT ART

13 bookartbookshop
17 Pitfield Street

An area as steeped in creativity as Shoreditch would not be complete without a funky bookshop devoted to the subject. Whimsical, authoritative and up-to-date publications keep track of the latest trends in the ever-changing world of contemporary art.

ENGLISH INTERIORS

14 Geffrye Museum
Kingsland Road

Interior design and history buffs will not be disappointed in Britain's only museum dedicated to English domestic furniture and decoration, housed in 18th-century almshouses, with a striking 1998 addition by Branson Coates. The Geffrye's comprehensive collection is displayed in a chronological sequence of re-created period

rooms, beginning with a 17th-century oak-panelled vignette, through the refined Georgian period, up to mid-century modern and contemporary interiors.

FROM VEGETABLES TO VINTAGE
15 Spitalfields Market
Commercial Street

One of London's liveliest and most varied markets, old Spitalfields contains everything from antiques to jewelry and textiles created by design-school graduates. A market was first held in the 13th century in the fields near St Mary Spital hospital and fruit and vegetables continued to be sold in the same area until 1991, when the market was relocated. Since then the Victorian structure and 1920s extension have been preserved (though under constant threat of demolition) as an indoor space for stall-holders selling organic produce, ethnic foods, fresh bread, as well as crafts, second-hand clothes and wooden toys. The best day to catch the full range of goods is on Sunday.

HAWKSMOOR'S TRIUMPH
16 Christ Church, Spitalfields
Commercial Street

Christ Church is considered one of the best churches designed by Nicholas Hawksmoor, the eccentric successor to Christopher Wren and subject of a fictionalized biography by celebrated London author Peter Ackroyd. Designed in 1714 directly opposite Spitalfields market, it has an outsized tower and sober spire that are classic idiosyncratic Hawksmoor features in what is often called the English Baroque. The church is largely intact, despite having been struck by lightning in 1841 and subsequently 'repaired'. With its four great Tuscan-style columns, the portico makes a grand entrance while the interior follows a simple, graceful design.

Three former antiques dealers have taken a spot of the dark and weary Bethnal Green Road and shined it up like a new and brightly coloured jewel. The interiors are a riot of decorative motifs all mixed and matched: a stuffed tiger and alligator, opulent chandeliers, bits of costume jewelry. However, the menu reflects a lot more focus: traditional French-inspired dishes from foie gras and duck breast to tiger prawns. It may be a little hard to focus on the food with décor such as this, but the experience will be indelible.

One of the bright, funky boutiques that are so much a part of the fabric of Shoreditch, Wink is small and lovingly formed. With a stand-out purple frontage and name spelled in white lightbulbs, the shop offers customized T-shirts, dainty tops and bottoms, as well as the leading edge of the young London fashion design scene.

Some of his pieces are available in Selfridge's (p. 168), but this is the only retail source for the complete Pauric Sweeney. An Irish designer with a taste for collage, he first found success as a jewelry designer but soon became known for his women's fashion collection, first shown at the Louvre in 2000. He's been a Shoreditch resident since 1996, and when he opened his shop in 1999 his collections were an immediate hit. Sweeney sells his own-design jewelry, as well as bags, belts and ready-to-wear in a style he describes as gothic. Recently, his customized Adidas track suits caught the attention of Madonna, who bought the entire collection.

The name is an acronym for the London Architectural Salvage and Supply Co. Ltd, and since 1979 it has been a unique source of architectural and ornamental antiques. Lassco are the lucky ones who are called when a demolition or refurbishment of a historic property is about to take place. In their Victorian church premises garden cherubs, church pews, stone gargoyles from building façades, stained glass-windows and entire carved doorways can be found among the amazing stock of items that they have purchased from such historic buildings as Buckingham Palace, the Tower of London, the Palace of Westminster, the Royal Opera House, the Victoria and Albert Museum and Kew Gardens.

California artist Dennis Severs fell in love with Spitalfields and its history, but his stunning re-creation of early-18th-century life in a London townhouse is an experience unlike any historic or museum study. Severs lived in the house, which he saved from dereliction, with all the trappings of the period, and until his death in 1999 personally escorted guests and visitors around the house in a complete sensory experience. Using everything from period furnishings and art, clothes, utensils and food, he aimed to 'bombard your senses'. 'I will get the 20th century out of your eyes, ears and everything,' he said. The house remains open to occasional tours, and each one is like a journey into an old-master painting. Meandering silently through the candlelit rooms during evening tours, you are transported far beyond historical reconstruction.

South Bank
Southwark
Bermondsey

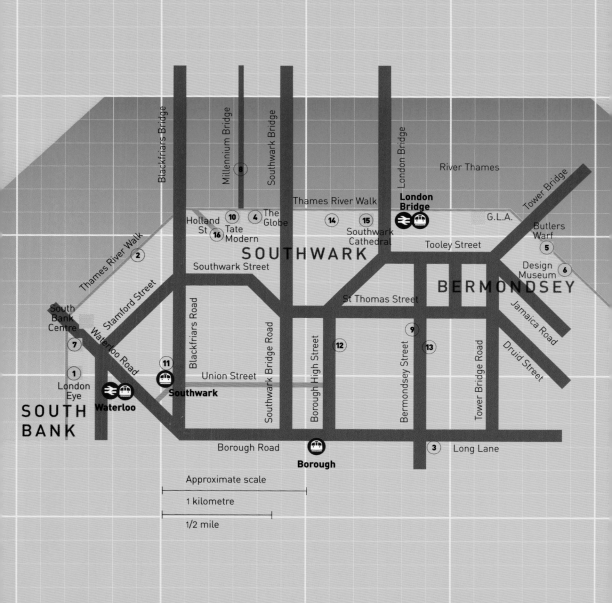

A string of new developments, which have stop-started since the 1980s and finally culminated in the opening of Tate Modern in 2000, have finally galvanized the South Bank into an area greater than the sum of its parts. Until such large-scale and high-profile cultural projects as the Tate and Globe Theatre gave locals and visitors a reason to head south in significant numbers, efforts to rehabilitate the riverine environments, such as the South Bank Centre, Butlers Wharf and the Design Museum, had been isolated and never really gained a critical mass. But what were once noble if disparate ventures are celebrated today as a 'string of pearls'. The London Eye, a terrific testimony to British design and engineering, and the ovoid Greater London Authority building designed by Norman Foster are fitting symbols of the South Bank's arrival. The Thames River Walk on the south provides spectacular views to the regal north shore as well as allowing a glimpse into a genuinely different side of London on the south.

Large-scale new building developments and local regeneration have in turn gradually been revivifying areas that had fallen into decay. The area immediately behind the Tate, usually referred to as Borough, is seeing an explosion of loft developments, and design studios have been flooding the area. Local markets, such as Borough (for fruit, vegetables and speciality food items) and Bermondsey (antiques), which have been operating for decades, if not centuries, are now attracting a more affluent clientele and international visitors. Giving speculative developers something to think about, the cooperative building Oxo Tower symbolizes local community spirit while promoting design talent and innovative crafts. And the completion of the Millennium Bridge has provided further stimulus: lunching City bankers and visitors to St Paul's can stroll effortlessly across the Thames to another world.

Compared with other parts of London, there are still relatively few places for stylish eating and drinking, but this is beginning to change as more and more design- and fashion-conscious taste-makers enter the area. Arty cafés (such as Delfina, p. 104), galleries, even gastro-pubs are beginning to pop up – and most appear to have staying-power (though there is as yet no hotel that caters to the chic or cultured). As you wander down the Thames River Walk, you may be tempted to eat at one of the museum restaurants – some of which are very good indeed, like the People's Palace in the South Bank Centre (p. 102) – but it's often worth the detour to find the locales that cater to the groovy residents rather than the tourists.

1 London Eye

Jubilee Gardens

It was a less-publicized and non-government-funded millennium project, but it must be the most enduringly successful in terms of public enjoyment. Standing in front of the new Jubilee Gardens between the Royal Festival Hall and the County Hall and conceived by architects David Marks and Julia Barfield, the graceful giant of a ferris wheel is a true marriage of design and engineering. Each glass-enclosed pod carries around 20 people and allows for uninterrupted views from its top height at 135 metres (450 feet) above the Thames. It takes 30 minutes for a full rotation of the 32 capsules, which means that the thrill of the ride is all in the eye.

2 Oxo Tower

Bargehouse Street

Before 1996, the places where you could have a good meal and enjoy a panoramic view of the Thames were virtually nonexistent. The Oxo Tower redevelopment, the felicitous victory of a neighbourhood coalition over hungry developers, changed all that when its top-floor restaurant and brasserie (designed by Lifshutz Davidson) opened (in association with posh department store Harvey Nichols) in the old tower building formerly belonging to the makers of bouillon cubes. The building now combines low-rent housing with retail design studios for 33 designers and makers on the first and second floors. The restaurant and brasserie-bar have breathtaking views and an open-air terrace. Prices tend to relate to the view rather than the food, so, given the choice, the brasserie's changing global menu is a better bet.

LEGENDARY ANTIQUES

3 Bermondsey Market
Bermondsey Square

This pre-dawn, Friday-only market held in a quiet square has legendary status among Londoners. The enchantment has to do with its early opening hours, a consequence, it is generally believed, of the fact that objects sold before sunrise are not subject to laws regarding handling of stolen goods. The reality is that this is London's most vibrant antiques market, a feeding ground mostly for dealers and knowledgable early risers – prices do so after 9 am. Jewelry and silver are the mainstays of the market, but paintings, china, rugs and a host of bric-à-brac are all to be had for the right, often negotiable, sum.

HAPPY RECREATION

4 Shakespeare's Globe
Bankside

American actor Sam Wanamaker's dream to re-create Shakespeare's Globe Theatre was realized in 1997. Complete with open-air wood stage and galleries, thatched roof and uncovered 'yard' – the standing area where the 'groundlings' who paid a penny for their entry would have stood while drinking beer, munching peanuts and oranges and regularly heckling the actors on stage – is a faithful reconstruction of the original Elizabethan theatre. Visitors today can stand in the yard for around five pounds, the atmosphere is informal and the whole is a delightful achievement in time-travel. Wine and snacks can be taken into the theatre as visitors would have done at the time. Performances, many of which are true to their Elizabethan originals and highly regarded by theatre critics and public, take place in all weathers, despite the lack of a roof.

5 The Gastrodome
Shad Thames

Terence Conran has come a long way since setting up his furniture-making business in 1952. First came Habitat and the eponymous design shops, then he turned his hand to food, and the London dining experience has not been the same since. His row of restaurants and gourmet food shops along the south bank of the Thames helped spearhead the revitalization of the area, along with the establishment of the Design Museum (see next entry) and its Blue Print Café. Within a single enclave are the unabashedly British Butlers Wharf Chop House, the refined, French-influenced, seafood-oriented Pont de la Tour and the relaxed, Italophile Cantina del Ponte. Conran has ten other restaurants around London in established areas, but it is the Gastrodome's location amid former derelict riverside warehouses (now mainly lofts), with gorgeous views towards the Tower of London and the City, that makes it a world of its own.

HIGHLIGHTING DESIGN
6 The Design Museum
28 Shad Thames

Billed as 'the world's first museum dedicated to the study of contemporary design', the all-white Design Museum's collection and exhibitions keep the world of product design open and accessible to the general public. The 1989 opening of the modern-inspired museum had the added benefit of beginning a gentrification of Butlers Wharf, a former warehouse district on the Thames, which is now teeming with attractive riverside boutiques, shops and eateries. Today, under the dynamic directorship of Alice Rawsthorn, the Design Museum classic modern interiors present a broad spectrum of exhibitions, covering all facets of design, from graphics and product design to fashion and architecture. Testament to her vision have been recent exhibitions on France's darlings of furniture design, the Bourellec brothers, and 'When Isabella met Philip', on the hats Philip Treacy (p. 167) designed for fashion designer Isabella Blow. In addition to the exhibition spaces are a bookshop selling a range of desirable design objects and the Blue Print Café, which serves modern interpretations of 'comfort food' against stupendous views over the city.

MAGNET FOR THE ARTS
7 South Bank Centre
- People's Palace
- Royal Festival Hall
- Hayward Gallery

Although many decry the South Bank Centre's concrete brutalism, built as the centrepiece in 1951 for the forward-looking Festival of Britian, its position today as one of London's most important cultural attractions is undisputed. The flexible exhibition spaces of the Hayward Gallery, a somewhat later addition to the complex, are dedicated principally to shows of modern and contemporary art. With three auditoriums, temporary exhibition spaces and outdoor performances, the South Bank Centre is a constant hive of activity, but it has only been recently that one has been able to eat well there too. Located on the third level of the Royal Festival Hall is the People's Palace restaurant, a space of enormous proportions, with all the formality and sophistication of a stand-alone establishment. The dramatic and minimal room, designed by Allies & Morrison, has stunning views of the river and the city beyond along its 36-metre-long (120-foot) glass front, as well as a bar that affords a quieter drinking atmosphere than the more lively drinks area on ground level. The menu is purposely British modern and reasonably priced, with serving times organized around performance times.

ENGINEERING WONDER
8 Millennium Bridge
Bankside

A competition to build a pedestrian bridge spanning the Thames, the first in central London in over a century, to link the Tate Modern with St Paul's Cathedral has resulted in what must be the most dramatic and beautiful of London's bridges. Designed by Norman Foster in close collaboration with sculptor Anthony Caro and world-renowned engineering firm Arup, it is an artistic and engineering masterwork, which wasn't without its initial problems. The 325-metre-long (1070-foot) 'blade-like' shallow suspension bridge, an entirely new concept in suspension bridges, is open 24 hours a day. Walking across on a moonlit night after an evening at the Globe or dinner at the Tate Modern, heading towards the lighted magisterial form of St Paul's, is truly an exhilarating London experience. A stroll during the day is pretty uplifting too.

THE ARTFUL LUNCHER

9 Delfina

50 Bermondsey Street

Located on a characterful street that is slowly beginning to reflect the quarter's artistic disposition since the opening of Tate Modern, Delfina started out as a warehouse that had been converted into studio space for artists by patron Delfina Entrecanales. The café for resident artists soon became a popular lunchtime spot, and today it helps to support the studio programme and provides public exhibition space. Its white-walled surroundings are a fitting backdrop to the changing collection of artworks, and even the labels on the wine bottles are works of art, produced by Turner Prize–nominee Tacita Dean. Maria Eilia is the artist in the kitchen, producing modern Mediterranean dishes such as seared tuna and chorizo risotto, in a menu that changes fortnightly.

THE POWER OF ART

10 Tate Modern

Bankside

The former Bankside Power Station designed by Giles Gilbert Scott was opened in 1963 but by the 1990s was disused and regarded by many as an eyesore. Through the vision of Tate director Nicholas Serota and Swiss architects Herzog & de Meuron the massive building was transformed to house the collections that make up the Tate Modern, international art from 1900 to the present, including important works by Dalí, Picasso and Matisse, as well as contemporary artists. The brick shell was left and the interiors gutted to create huge open spaces. The former Turbine Hall, which runs the whole length of the vast building, makes a grand gallery entrance not unlike a cathedral space. In addition to the galleries, which feature permanent and temporary exhibitions, there are a café and art bookshop – the largest in Europe – on the ground floor. The top-floor restaurant, serving modern British cuisine, has glorious views over the Thames.

11 Baltic

74 Blackfriars Road

Sleek, stylish, modern and eastern European, Baltic has turned a contemporary eye to Slavic cuisine with a cool, tasteful design more often seen in the West End than south of the river. The tall, open interior was once a workshop for coach building, but has been stunningly remodelled. The inventive menu ranges from seasoned crayfish in vodka butter to venison with cherries, with dashes of caviar, beetroot and blinis in between. Service is as smooth as the interior decoration and low-amplitude jazz serenades the clientele venturing down from the financial district across the river. A slick bar serves a host of Polish vodkas and a spectrum of interesting, vodka-based cocktails.

12 The George Inn

77 Borough High Street

On a cobbled courtyard off Borough High Street is London's only surviving galleried coaching inn, a rare example of a medieval pub in the city. Destroyed by fire and rebuilt in 1676, it has escaped demolition many times and is now protected by the National Trust. Its distinctive whitewashed but yellowed walls, oak beams, wood panelling and lattice windows evoke another era beyond the modern-day traffic outside. Dickens is said to have been a regular in one of the series of room-sized bars that make up the ground floor. The former bedchambers upstairs have long since been converted to dining and public rooms but have lost none of their gloriously aged character in the transition.

13 Fashion and Textile Museum
83 Bermondsey Street

Extravagant fashion designer Zandra Rhodes and Mexican architect Ricardo Legorreta have conspired to shake up the brick lanes of Bermondsey with a new museum devoted to fashion. Legorreta's characteristic swathes of colour – bright orange and pink – do for building what Rhodes has done for fashion for decades. According to Rhodes, the museum is 'the first of its kind, to showcase the work of local and international fashion and textile designers'. It will also serve students in the industry by offering fellowships. This latest grand architectural project to grace the South Bank has an interior as striking as the exterior, with sculptural spaces in monochrome white, pink and blue.

CITY OF WINE
14 Vinopolis
1 Bank End

'Uncork your mind; indulge your senses' is the motto of this modern temple to the grape along the Millennium Mile on the South Bank of the Thames. A wine museum that features an interactive virtual tour through all the wine-growing regions of the world, it contains enough history and information to make you drunk on facts. Luckily there is also the revered product itself, available at tasting tables along the way and sold in the adjacent wine store. Even if you're just stopping by, there's a vast selection to be had by the glass or bottle in the Wine Wharf bar as well as in the Michelin-rated Cantina Vinopolis.

GOTHIC ORIGINAL
15 Southwark Cathedral
Montague Close

The earliest Gothic church in London was built as St Mary Overie in 1220 and became the parish church of St Saviour, Southwark, in 1539. It suffered fires and periods of neglect until it was bought from James I in 1614 by the parishioners, who have looked after it ever since. Happily, it was not damaged during the Civil War, and the current tower with four pinnacles was finished in 1689. Among the many wonderful tributes, monuments and gifts inside is a 13th-century carved oak effigy of a knight and another of John Gower, who was a friend to Chaucer and himself a poet (Chaucer's pilgrims in the *Canterbury Tales* set off from a spot near

here). Inside the southwest entrance the Gothic arcading is still visible, which was rebuilt after a fire in 1206. At one end of the north aisle are 12 ceiling bosses taken from the 15th-century wooden roof that collapsed in 1830. They depict vices such as malice, gluttony and falsehood, as well as heraldic sunflowers and roses. Piers, chancel and other elements from the 13th century survived, along with many wonderful later pieces, such as the carved monument to Alderman Humble and his wives, dressed in their 17th-century best. The monument to Shakespeare is 20th century, but there is a funeral paving stone belonging to the Bard's brother Edmund (d. 1607).

RARE AND OUT-OF-PRINT
16 Marcus Campbell Art Books
43 Holland Street

If your visit to the Tate Modern has sparked your interest in modern art, then you might want to wander over to Marcus Campbell, conveniently located across the street. Relocated from Piccadilly Arcade in 1998, Marcus Campbell specializes in books on late-20th-century art and artists, with a particular focus on rare and out-of-print artists' books by and about such figures as Sol LeWitt, Ed Ruscha, Marcel Broodthaers, Lawrence Weiner and Gilbert and George. 'Conceptual art when it began', Campbell says, and 'the historical stuff is what interests me'.

Style Traveller

sleep • eat • drink
shop • retreat

sleep

London's best hotels are famed for their discreet service and attention to detail. Although it was not until relatively recently that London responded to the global trend for stylish, more individualistic accommodation, there is now an incomparable array of establishments, ranging from the ultramodern to the ingeniously or ironically traditional. Here is a selection of the best hard-to-find hideaways, small (from three-room) mid-modern meccas, accessibly grand bolt-holes and over-the-top tributes to minimalism, their distinct character reflecting the charisma and vision of their founders.

72 **The Rookery**

2 Peter's Lane, Cowcross Street
From £190

It is hard to say what delights most about this hidden gem. There is the tricky access off a tree-shaded, pedestrianized alley near bustling Smithfield Market, before one steps across the threshold of what seems like someone's private house. Once inside, there are the 33 eccentrically appointed bedrooms, each named after a local character who once lived near by, thus imbuing the four Georgian houses that make up this quintesstially London townhouse hotel not only with period charm, but with real personality. Smithfield is an area that was once known for lawlessness – Charles Dickens's Fagin is said to have haunted its streets – being outside the City's jurisdiction. Areas such as these were known as 'rookeries' and though Smithfield is now full of smartly dressed City workers, clubbers and restaurant patrons, the edgy atmosphere has not completely disappeared, all of which makes for a rather irresistible mix of 'olde-worlde' intrigue and modern sophistication.

As you might expect, The Rookery is a labour of love, created by Douglas Bain and Peter McKay, who have artfully combined the old and new in a romantic, quirky but detail-conscious atmosphere. All of the modern amenities are on tap, while a careful refurbishment and restoration of the original furnishings and fittings that draws on Bain's and McKay's extensive antiques knowledge – wardrobes, secretaires, great carved four-poster beds or Gothic-style bedsteads, period oak panelling, even the Victorian commodes – have taken place with the idea that 'history is always more appealing when it has been cleaned up a bit'. Specialist craftsmen were hired to restore the period plumbing fixtures and adapt them to modern pipework.

The hotel's *pièce de résistance* is the incomparable 'Rook's Nest', a top-level suite with the same carefully honed period feel, enhanced by a restored Edwardian bathing machine, but with a hidden extra: the ceiling opens to reveal a rooftop sitting room accessed by a small stair where guests can enjoy their own private panorama of London. Downstairs, life is less heady, but no less luxurious.

The Sanderson

15 50 Berners Street
From £2oo

Nouvelle baroque, a study in white, a whimsical if not surreal medley in quirky furniture pieces housed in a protected 1960s office building – the ironic design element of Ian Schrager's seventh hotel masterpiece (and collaboration with Philippe Starck) is in its most exalted form just north of Soho. Indeed, according to Schrager, his 'urban spa' is one of his most daring and at times surprising enterprises, located in an unlikely edifice (the word 'Sanderson' is the only giveaway – even New York art director Fabien Baron couldn't do away with this vestige of preservation requirements) in an unlikely street populated by contract furniture sellers and accountants. Perhaps this is what elevates the Sanderson experience beyond the obvious and well-located appeal of other Schrager confections.

Tucked away beyond the lobby's 1970 Dalí 'Bocca' sofa, Louis XV–style furniture and Venetian mirrors are the Long Bar, a global destination bar complete with a 25-metre (80-foot) onyx bar and international food; Spoon + , the first import from celebrated Parisian superchef Alain Ducasse; and Agua, a diaphanous two-storey, 1000-square-metre (10,000-square-foot) spa sanctuary catering to the world-weary. Other delights and surprises lie behind the irreverent décor: an unexpected Eastern-inspired courtyard (also serving the restaurant) and a bamboo roof garden with views over the capital.

Guest rooms are perhaps variations on a theme of white, but that's no matter when the sheets have a 450-thread count; the mock sleigh beds are silver-leaved and bathroom areas obscured behind opaque silk drapes. Indeed, Starck's room designs are more a play of transparency and opacity (and vanity?) than anything else.

'Affordable chic in the heart of Knightsbridge' is how hoteliers and interior designers Tim and Kit Kemp describe their latest venture in London, a new take on a 'traditional English bed and breakfast'. Kit Kemp is no amateur designer, having imbued the Covent Garden, the Charlotte Street and the Pelham with her particularly tasteful and eclectic blend of modern and traditional English style. The Knightsbridge she describes as 'fresh, modern English', which is discerned through the specially commissioned fabrics and artwork set off by comfortably traditional sofas, chairs and tables.

There are 44 rooms here, and all have been individually designed by Kit Kemp, so they are rich in colour, pattern and texture. There is the 'fuschia room', a room draped in pale greens and deep purples, as well as some with more neutral tones but still bearing light floral touches. Kit Kemp's trademark retro-design Roberts radios are in every room. Her quirky dress mannequins, which she upholsters in varying fabrics, appear in large and small versions, adding to the overall character and charm.

Although there is no restaurant on-site, there is 24-hour room service with a gourmet menu. Continental breakfast is usually taken by room service, though guests can choose to eat in the jungle-themed drawing room or the library, both of which feature outstanding works of British art commissioned for the hotel.

COOL CONVENIENCE

No. 5 Maddox Street

5 Maddox Street
From £235

Located on a typical upmarket Mayfair street running between Bond and Regent Streets, No. 5 Maddox Street is an exceptionally conceived, 12-suite hotel that focuses resolutely on the idea of a modern sanctuary. In contrast to the surrounding galleries, upscale shops and auction houses promoting largely classic values, the aim here is to transport the visitor to another realm, one tinged by Eastern themes and ideals of relaxation.

More of a luxurious serviced apartment than a traditional hotel – all of the one-, two- and three-bedroom suites have fully equipped kitchens, and chefs can be brought in for intimate in-suite entertaining – there is everything the traveller needs for a home away from home. Enveloped by dark browns and natural tones, animated bamboo, tropical plantings and lively flower displays, this is not your average urban retreat.

Each of the suites has its own chic appeal – the dual-level mezzanine loft suite has top-floor views over London, the enormous one-bedroom deluxe suite its own terrace, the two-bedroom loft suite features a leather staircase leading to the master bedroom – but surpassing all of them is the Bartlett Suite, with three double bedrooms, two baths and two terraces that can accommodate a team of creatives or a large family. All suites also have bamboo floors, sable bedcovers, living-dining room and all of the technical amenities the digital global traveller has come to expect.

Barely noticeable from the street – no doorman, no overt entrance – No. 5 caters to people who tire of having to eat out every meal or retire in the same public rooms. While the room rates are above average for London (though not for this area), guests can economize by cooking for themselves, for example, or by enjoying their private views rather than cocktails in the bar. In the bustling centre of London, No. 5 offers oases of self-sufficient calm, a place to call your own, for business or pleasure.

'In art, in taste, in life, in speech, you decide from feeling, and not from reason.' So wrote the great essayist, critic and Napoleon biographer William Hazlitt in 1822. With such inspiration in mind, Douglas Bain and Peter McKay set out to create a home away from home in a set of three of Soho's most characterful houses, built in 1718 and where Hazlitt died, purportedly of drinking too much tea, on 18 September 1830 in what was then a boarding house. Set on a bustling street and surrounded by creative agencies, restaurants and bars, Hazlitt's is a world away from 21st-century global London, a discreet and intimate hideaway from the modern world. Guests who desire a long-lost quintessentially English experience will experience the words that Hazlitt requested for his gravestone, GRATEFUL AND CONTENTED.

But don't let the 23 rooms' carved mahogany four-poster beds, Victorian claw-foot tubs (some original to the house), the rich, bold colours of the walls and fabrics (the hotel was completely remodelled in 2001), the small sitting rooms and wonky floors and the absence of elevators fool you, this is the haunt of the media, antiques collectors and dignitaries who sense that there is something very special about Hazlitt's and far removed from corporate modern. The staff might be stylish and amenities contemporary, but the contrast wouldn't have bothered Hazlitt, who observed, 'We are not hypocrites in our sleep.'

86 **Threadneedles**

6 5 Threadneedle Street

From £275

Threadneedle Street is named for either the three needles that are in the arms of the Needlemakers' Company guild symbol or for the Merchant Tailors who were chartered in 1327 but were functioning long before. Located directly behind the Bank of England in the City's Square Mile, Threadneedles elegantly fills a former banking hall designed by William and Andrew Moseley in 1856 and achieves the delicate balance of reconciling corporate contemporary with a genuine and rather spectacular feat of architectural restoration. Everything has been carefully refurbished, but the centrepiece is unquestionably the stunning painted-glass dome that hovers over the lobby area. Grand architectural features such as the domed entrance hall, with its Corinthian capitals, dentil moulding, neo-Classical frieze and delicate painted glass have been retained, restored and humanized by low-level lighting, snug upholstered chairs and shelves filled with books and objects.

As you would expect, rooms from the smallest standard double to the four-bedroom suite are appointed with full electronic gear, bathrooms tiled in limestone and soft-toned furnishings to encourage a calming atmosphere after a frenetic day making financial deals or visiting Christopher Wren churches. Though there are corporate tendencies in somewhat anonymous hallways, flashes of neon here and there, fresh flowers, the occasional floral design flourish and vibrant contemporary keep the business feel at bay. Truly rare in the City, Threadneedles is a small high-quality individualized hotel that places great value on personal service for demanding guests and a location near the centre of historic London. There might be a lot of suits in the bar and restaurant, but you can always slip upstairs and arrange for champagne, strawberries and cream or a glass of cognac and biscotti to enjoy in the bath.

28 **Eleven Cadogan Gardens**
24 11 Cadogan Gardens
From £160

A stone's throw from Sloane Square, marked only by a single sign 'No. 11', Eleven Cadogan Gardens is a genuine late-Victorian testament to what makes the English hotel unique: understatement, discretion, an apparently undesigned interior that works wonderfully, and a just a hint of the aristocratic. It's not hard to understand why it is reportedly design guru Philippe Starck's favourite London hotel. Though one must resist the urge to use superlatives (particularly inappropriate in this context), there is an authenticity, warmth and ease that makes a stay at Eleven Cadogan Gardens an experience you would have only here, in the heart of Chelsea, which means that the high volume of loyal repeat guests can make getting a room tricky at times.

Today's establishment began life in the late 19th century, when Lord Chelsea built four mansions on his cricket ground near Buckingham Palace, which soon become London's first private townhouse hotel. Today, there remain 60 rooms (ask for ones at the back, which overlook beautifully manicured gardens), rich wood-panelled walls, oil paintings, an oak staircase and countless antiques, along with two Garden Suites, one that offers a private entrance and the other featuring a large drawing room that overlooks the garden.

There is no reception desk, but a butler greets visitors at the door, signifying the level of service to follow. Guests handsign a well-worn ledger before being escorted to their premises. Tucked discreetly away in the building are modern amenities, such as a gym and beauty treatment room, reluctant concessions, no doubt, to contemporary travellers. To round out the picture, guests are offered afternoon tea in the dining room, along with fresh cakes, sherry and canapes – what else?

West Street

13–15 West Street
From £250

The small, detail-conscious boutique hotel has just got smaller and even more finely wrought – the micro-hotel has arrived in the heart of London's Covent Garden theatre district. Just off the patchy Shaftesbury Avenue is an unexpected delight, artfully concealed to all but a few lucky member-guests. With only three suites designed by hip London architects Sally Mackereth and James Wells, the hotel focuses on quality of experience, location and vibe rather than quantity of rooms and amenities.

The hotel is the brainchild of Christopher Bodker, Rowley Leigh and Marian Scrutton, whose success with such restaurants as Circus (p. 50) and The Avenue (p. 135) have placed them among London's most discerning epicureans. Housed in a building formerly used by Japanese businessmen for dubious exploits, the restaurant and bar occupy the ground and basement floors and three highly individualized suites on the floors above.

The high-gloss White Room features white Carrara marble flooring, red accents in soft and hard furnishing and Constanza lamps. The Stone Room (more a suite) takes its name from the limestone and earthy elements – deep browns, leather, creams – and boasts a fabulous private terrace large enough (70 square metres [700 square feet]) for a good-sized cocktail party and features a private lift. And the double-height Loft, occupying the entire fourth floor, has dark oak floors, green-slate walls and bathroom and bright-orange Tulip chairs designed by Geoffrey Bernett, one of many flourishes that dot these sophisticated chambers.

With the Blue Room – a high-tech screening room – the downstairs bar and its magical 6-metre (20-foot) kinetic sculpture by Richard Clark and Alex MacGregor and a restaurant serving modern Mediterranean cuisine, there's little doubt that size – exquisitely detailed – is everything.

14 **Miller's Residence**

11 111A Westbourne Grove
From £160

While many small hotels struggle to attain that authentic period feel, Martin Miller's small but opulently decorated residence in Notting Hill is overflowing with the real thing: Miller is the name behind *Miller's Antique Price Guide* (previously the *Lyle Antiques Review*), which he and a partner started in 1969 when there was no published listing of antiques prices. His knowledge of antique objects and furnishings is unquestionable, as is his taste for what he calls 'throwing things together'. His casual attitude towards items that most people would perceive as precious or untouchable is part of what makes Miller's so attractive to a broad clientele ranging from antiques hunters scouring Notting Hill's shops to the fashion and media set.

This is Miller's own residence, opened to guests since 1997, and he has filled it with things that he has acquired over the years, 'a mix of everything from 17th century to early 20th', he says, 'but it has that very Victorian feeling, very full, that sense of "when did you last see the wallpaper?"'. Miller doesn't adhere to a particular style, but prefers a feeling enhanced by 'open fireplaces, candles and low-lighting', an approach that won his previous hotel, a 17th-century timbered house called Chilston Park, which he ran with his former wife, Judith, the award of Romantic Hotel of the Year. It's an accolade Miller values more than a Michelin star and perhaps why he named each of the six rooms and suites in this hotel after the Romantic poets and decorated them in the spirit of each: Venetian paintings and Italian decoration in the Byron room, rich red fabrics in the Keats room and calming floral patterns in the Browning room. But that is as far as any rules go. A stay at Miller's is like staying with friends: 'it's smaller than a hotel, but it's much more than a B & B,' Miller explains, 'we're good at getting people into clubs, restaurants, etc. We offer the same service, if not better,' he says with a laugh, 'as a five-star concierge. We have good contacts.' They also have a good feeling about their guests, who are invited to help themselves to drinks and snacks from the well-stocked kitchen at any time of day or night, all of which are included in the price.

eat

In the past, few visitors would have seen London as a culinary destination, but that has changed radically over the past ten years. A variety of ethnic restaurants has also been an aspect of the city's cosmopolitanism, but today offers more choice than ever before — everything from European cuisine at the very highest level to exotic fare updated with Western touches. Where London has seen the most notable — and, for the world gourmand, most intriguing — development is in the celebration of its own culinary traditions. Where once the visitor faced 'pub grub', today there are 'gastro-pubs' — bars serving well-prepared dishes using fresh local ingredients — and New British cuisine tailored to today's more international and demanding palettes.

42

Momo

17 25 Heddon Street

Many say it's all about atmosphere at this unexpected shrine to North African food and décor in Mayfair, but Momo is much more than that. Sandwiched between the Regency façades of Regent Street and sartorial Savile Row is another world dedicated to suffusing the senses with exoticism and extravagance – the contrast couldn't be more London. It would all feel rather themed, had Momo not been the product of Mourad Mazouz, whose own travels account for many of the objects that provide the backdrop to the elevated Maghreb (Moroccan, Tunisian, Algerian) cuisine. Look out for echouia salad with chickpea croquettes; vegetable soup with saffron and lemon; sweet and spicy pigeon pie with almonds and cumin. For those in search of less full-on immersion, Casablanca can be experienced remotely in the adjacent tea-room. Below is Kemia, a favourite of princes and princesses from near and far and one of London's more desirable nightspots, for members only Thursday to Saturday but open 'by invitation' on other nights.

LATE-NIGHT DINING STYLE

86 **Home**

25 100–106 Leonard Street

What began as a groovy downstairs DJ bar a few years ago with a single room serving Mediterranean fare to the early inhabitants of the Shoreditch regeneration has burgeoned into a fully fledged, glass-fronted hip bar and restaurant serving the now more established bohemian elements of the area with a dose of bankers migrating from the City just south. Like the seemingly ad-hoc arrangement of mid-century furniture, the international eclectic cuisine of the busy restaurant caters to a broad range of customers, tastes and serving times (until 1 am). A good first stop before hitting the bars of Hoxton Square (p. 159) and environs or a resuscitating last stop, Home is a neighbourhood joint that feels local and buzzes with the knowing locals and appreciative guests.

EASTERN BEAUTY

60 **Hakkasan**

18 8 Hanway Place

As you make your way from the teeming throngs of Tottenham Court Road and Oxford Street, down a rather unsavoury alleyway, nothing can prepare you for this exquisite bar and restaurant, which combines stylish modern-exotic design with a delicate Singaporean-tinged cuisine. Through the doors you step out of a gritty urban backstreet, down into a seductively lit, slate-lined stair and into a sensuous aquamarine environment masterfully created by French designer Christian Liaigre. London's fashionable set prefer to queue for the evening scene, but the best time to go is at lunch, when a modern Dim Sum menu, prepared by head chef Tong Chee Hwee (formerly of Summer Pavilion at Singapore's Ritz Carlton), is available against purple-illuminated glass, fretted-wood partitions and dark wood – continents away from London and worlds away from the mass retail frenzy above. You needn't stop at Dim Sum, for a more complete, contemporary Chinese menu for lunch and dinner is available, as are Asian-tinted cocktails conceived by one of London's master mixers.

Rules

35 Maiden Lane

Claiming to be London's oldest restaurant, Rules has been going continuously since Thomas Rule first opened it in 1798, when it was known for its 'porter, pies and oysters'. Over the centuries, royalty and celebrity have filled its room: it was known as the haunt of Edward VII Prince of Wales and his mistress, the actress Lily Langtry, who made such a habit of visiting that a private door was added so they could avoid the prying eyes of the public; Charles Dickens, Graham Greene and H. G. Wells were frequent diners. It is still devoted to distinctly British meat and game – rabbit, deer, grouse and the prized Belted Galloway cattle – which comes directly from the restaurant's own estates in Lartington in England's High Pennines to ensure the highest standards. A recently restored and beautifully atmospheric dining room, preserved by the last of only three owning families over the decades, provides handsomely for the 'rakes, dandies and superior intelligences who comprise its clientele'. Living London culture and history are alive and well in Covent Garden.

42

The Avenue

16 7–9 St James's Street

Designed by London-based American architect Rick Mather, the Avenue consciously strives 'to bring the quality, energy and style, typical of restaurants in New York, to London'. Since its opening in 1995, however, the Avenue has achieved a style all its own among its discerning Mayfair clientele. A long, glowing, glass-topped bar marks the entrance to a spare, minimalist space beneath a skylit ceiling. The menu, as described by its chef, is modern European with 'no frills, no fuss' and changes seasonally. Therefore, despite the high-end atmosphere, they happily serve a range from foie gras to fish fingers. The wine list is international with an emphasis on Burgundies, and special selections are obtained at auction from Christie's, located nearby.

TOWNHOUSE DINING

42

Lindsay House

29 21 Romilly Street

Irish chef Richard Corrigan was awarded a Michelin star for his restaurant, which occupies a 1740 London townhouse in the heart of Soho. Though set in an atmopshere of cheap Italian cafés, pubs and sex shops, the genteel and serene atmosphere of the Lindsay House – which begins as soon as you ring the entrance doorbell – sits in genteel contrast to the revelling hoi polloi outside. Two Georgian dining rooms, with preserved period details, high ceilings and minimally added decoration, have an elegantly at-home feel about them, which, despite the high ratio of staff to diners, makes for a warm, intimate and ultimately romantic experience. The menu encompasses a range of lightly fused cuisines from gazpacho of English crayfish to guinea fowl in Madeira, and the wine list is varied and well suited to the exquisitely prepared dishes.

ARCHETYPAL CARVERY

42 The Grill Room at The Dorchester

7 53 Park Lane

It's really a shame to visit London without splashing out for a proper carvery in one of the classic grand hotel restaurants. Merely uttering 'The Dorchester' carries a ring of refinement that becomes evident beneath the great Grill Room's gold-leaf-lined, coffered ceiling and among the leather armchairs, velvet curtains and Flemish tapestries, all of which are of the 1931 room, when it was known as the Spanish Grill and featured a dedicated sherry bar. Today, the menu celebrates high British cuisine. Head chef Henri Brosi, who came to the Grill Room in 1999 after a period at Claridge's, has embraced the traditional fare with a passion. The grilled dishes include steaks, Scottish lobster, wild salmon and turbot, complemented by such old favourites as roast Aberdeenshire beef with Yorkshire pudding and humble shepherd's pie. Brosi's signature dishes are variations on the traditional – scallops with warm tomato and saffron dressing, or rack of lamb with mustard and herb crust. Having had only seven chefs in the last 70 years, the Grill Room stands as a timeless and unwavering London institution.

ART DÉCO MASTERPIECE

42 **Claridge's**

25 55 Brook Street

Former footballer Gordon Ramsay is enjoying a reputation as London's finest and currently only three-Michelin-starred chef. His past successes – Aubergine, Pétrus, among others – have given him ample experience to take on the restaurant in a venerated London hotel celebrating nearly 200 years of refined hospitality. The august five-star hotel started out as elite as it remains, being designed to accommodate foreign royalty and nobility 'with the discretion of a private house'. Under the direction of Ramsay, the restaurant, serving principally New French with exceptionally well-orchestrated service in a lush Art Déco setting, has caused a ripple of excitement in the world of haute cuisine; it is often booked weeks in advance. This is a restaurant for a very special experience, but one that can be made accessible to many by the well-priced prix-fixe menus at lunch and dinner. Before dinner one might have a cocktail at the lovely Déco bar, which draws local gallerists and auctioneers after work, or, after dinner, at the Fumoir, an elegant cigar-smoker's paradise.

The Cow, at the periphery of Notting Hill, was a pleasant old-fashioned pub even before it became known for its new menu and speciality, fresh seafood. Owned by Tom Conran, son of restaurateur and design guru Terence, today it is a little pub with a large following and a jolly place to meet for a drink and a plate of oysters, a little slice of Notting Hill life and a favourite of locals despite the occasional visit from a celebrity (Elvis Costello, Uma Thurman, Kylie Minogue and Hugh Grant have stopped by). If a heartier meal is in your sights, you can have a proper repast in the intimate upstairs dining room, which focuses on modern British (you are advised to book ahead). In nice weather, sitting outside on the quiet road in view of the nearby Westbourne (p. 20) you might feel a little spoiled for choice.

Hailed as the first 'gastro-pub' in London, the Eagle began in 1991 what many modernized London pubs are now trying to do with widely varying degrees of success. As owner Michael Belben, who started The Eagle with David Eyre, the Eagle's first chef, says, 'we weren't the first pub to serve good food, but we were probably the first pub to serve extremely good food in casual surroundings'. What they did not want to do was 'exclude traditional drinkers'; nor did they want to include a lot of 'unnecessary trimmings'. So you won't find table linens or complicated selections of courses or even a tab (you pay when you order), but you will find a place that's welcoming for a long drink or a very good dinner, as enjoyed by the nearby journalists and creatives. Wood details and an eclectic mix of well-worn leather sofas, old bar stools and unmatched dining chairs contribute to the casual atmosphere. The daily-changing menu is hearty and leans toward the Mediterranean, though current chef Tom Norrington-Davis says this is because they serve what they think is good, not because they're adhering to style.

All-white tablecloths and high-backed chairs arranged against magnificent soaring white walls in what used to be the 1897 Westminster Library, the Cinnamon Club is the modern, upscale face of Indian food as envisioned by owner Iqbal Wahhab. Original bookshelves, wood screens and parquet flooring have been retained while Indian marble and stone have been incorporated into a clean-lined fusion of colonial convergence. Under chef Vivek Singh with the help of Michelin-starred French chef Eric Chavot, contemporary Indian cuisine reaches new heights of sophistication and refinement, served to a public ranging from Westminster politicians to jetsetters. Traditional techniques are applied to unconventional ingredients and vice versa, producing consistently acclaimed dishes such as sweet potato cake with crispy okra and spiced yoghurt, duck breast with sesame tamarind sauce and spinach dumplings with chickpea cake, all suggesting that this is a place with staying-power. The downstairs late-night and members' bar and lounge serves up a collection of Indian-tinged cocktails and dance music to ensure your evening ends on a cool note.

Probably the most ambitious and chicest venues to open in the last decade, Sketch – so-called because it is constantly evolving – marks the apotheosis of high design, high style and high gastronomy. A long-term labour of love and passion by Mourad Mazouz (see also p. 132) and set in a Georgian mansion most recently occupied by Christian Dior, Sketch displays a dazzling diversity of design that extends to a parlour, art gallery, two bars, two restaurants and a lecture theatre. No surface has been left unconsidered – from the Swarovski-bejewelled bathrooms to the in-situ artworks; no culinary delight thought too extravagant – Parisian masterchef Pierre Gagnaire has created all the food, from the pastries in the parlour to the Library restaurant's haute cuisine (probably the most expensive in Britain); no possibility for design overlooked – from the carts in the Gallery restaurant by Marc Newson and the East Bar's toilet pods to the custom furniture pieces by Noe Duchaufour Lawrance. A total work of art for all the senses, Sketch sets new standards in the urban epicurean experience.

Smiths of Smithfield

67–77 Charterhouse Street

Smiths sits facing the old cattle market, Smithfields, and if you were expecting beef then you won't be disappointed. John Torode (formerly of Quaglino's and Mezzo) has embraced traditional British food and spruced it up with Thai and Italian touches using fresh ingredients. He began by sourcing rare and organic breeds in Britain for his meat and poultry dishes, and he buys organic produce whenever possible. The former meatpacking warehouse he chose as a venue is historic, with a large, informal ground floor filled with refectory tables that serves breakfast all day long. On the first floor is a red-leather-boothed cocktail bar to lubricate the way to the second-floor dining room, an informal seated service. The Top Floor is the showpiece for Torode's rare and organic breed dishes: Gloucester Old pot pork fillet with bok choi, crab ravioli and Thai broth; or Welsh black sirloin (aged 26 days). A veritable temple to the best of British meat and seafood, Smiths offers several types of dining experience depending on your mood, company and hunger. A new London institution.

A shining example of high-style Indian cuisine – 'the Mother of Indian restaurants' it was dubbed by one publication in the know – even before its relaunch in 2000 (after being destroyed by a fire), what was once a classic has reinvented itself with an even greater commitment to contemporary cuisine, style and service. The recent reincarnation pays homage to the original Red Fort, built in Delhi by Shah Jahan, who also built the Taj Mahal, by incorporating the same materials but updated to contemporary demands in a lush and sultry setting. The menu is produced by chef Mohammed Rais, who comes from a 300-year line of court chefs and who has mastered the art of *dum pukht*, a form of steam cooking, which imbues regional biryanis with an added edge. A wide selection of refined dishes includes *dum ka* lobster, which has been steamed in cumin-infused broth, and *murgh mussalam*, poussin with Kashmiri chilies and browned onions. Downstairs is Akbar (p. 158), much more than just a restaurant cocktail lounge.

QUIET AND CLUBBY
[42] **Adam Street**
[51] 8 Adam Street
Lunch only (for non-members)

Like the most intriguing city addresses, you wouldn't know it was there unless you were looking for it. A plaque announces a private members' club just off the Strand, and the bell suggests the uninvited are not to wander in. Fortunately you don't have to be a member to book a table in the restaurant for lunch, though descending the red-carpeted staircase does deliver the zing of exclusivity. As you step into the subterranean space, you might remember that the dual barrel vaults in which the restaurant and bar are now situated were the foundations of the Adelphi, a development of artists' residences conceived and partly built by master architects Robert and James Adam from 1768 to 1792. Today the space has been modernized, peopled with nearby publishers and features a bar area, with contemporary club chairs and purple velvet stools, while the restaurant is a formal, intimate dining space with classic British dishes (including a revisited macaroni and cheese). A destination after morning gallery visits on Trafalgar Square.

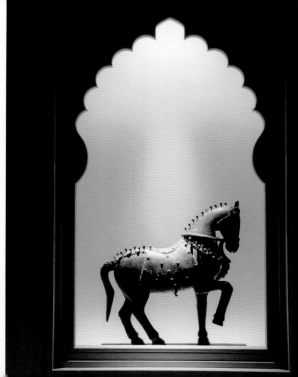

One of only two Indian restaurants in England to have achieved a Michelin star, Zaika is the winning marriage of restaurateur Claudio Pulze and prize-winning chef Vineet Bhatia. Recently relocated to exotically inflected historic premises just off Hyde Park in Kensington, Zaika – which means 'sophisticated flavours' – presents classical dishes with new and inventive twists that are destined to redefine ethnic cuisine. The elegant setting is an ideal accompaniment to the refined dishes. Served with élan amid lush colours, contemporary Indian motifs and a stylish bar, dishes include Bhatia's signature *dhungar machli tikka/murghabhi seekhe*, minced duck roll and tandoori-smoked salmon flavoured with mustard and dill; *tikhe machli,* pan-fried, spice-marinated sea bass with Indian couscous, raw mango and turmeric sauce; and *samundri khazana,* crispy Hawaiian soft-shell crab, seared, spiced scallops with Indian risotto, spring onions and green herb sauce

72 **St John**

5 26 St John Street

Located a stone's throw from Smithfield Market, where livestock was traded for some 200 years, St John is a symbol of the British love affair with meat. This association, according to Trevor Gulliver, who started the restaurant with chef Fergus Henderson in 1994, happened somewhat by accident. True, one of the most famous and photographed items on their menu is bone marrow served with toasted flat bread and parsley salad, but this is more a reflection of the quality of the cuisine than a commitment to meat-eating. But St John also prides itself on its relationship with farmer-producers, its fresh-baked bread (which can be bought from the bakery) and the fact that they butcher their own meat, which gives them the opportunity and, they feel, an obligation to use all the parts. With a staunchly loyal following that includes dozens who ask for the menu to be faxed to them daily (some just so they can find out when tripe is being served), it is not hard to be won over by Gulliver's belief that 'a good restaurant is like a good friend'. The stark, whitewashed premises – which included a former smokehouse – complement the food perfectly.

NEW CULINARY FORMS

86 Eyre Brothers
24 70 Leonard Street

Having redefined pub-grub and British cooking to respectable and now ubiquitously imitated level, David Eyre and his brother Robert are the gastro-publicans par excellence. In the constantly evolving creative sphere that is the Shoreditch area, David Eyre has taken the Mediterranean-inspired dishes he explored in his former environs into a new realm, with a more formal, indeed sleek, new restaurant that focuses largely on Iberian ingredients and flavours, with a dash of Mozambique, where the Eyres grew up. The warm but vaguely retro décor features chairs originally designed for Harry's Bar, mahogany floors and low ceilings, which have proved popular for power lunchers from the financial district nearby and welcoming to a diverse crowd in the evenings. Now starting to appear on international restaurant-destination lists, Eyre Brothers offers dishes that include pheasant casserole with dried ceps, Mozambique prawns *piri-piri* and the Alentejo fish stew.

drink

When people think of London, they think of pubs. And while there are beautiful and characterful public houses throughout the city, those of great individual style are rare but well worth a detour. Today, however, pubs are only part of the story. Fuelled by London's famed club culture, its status as a magnet in the global design scene and more relaxed laws on drinking hours, chic watering holes are establishing themselves everywhere. And after a couple of centuries of tea hegemony, coffee culture has re-entered London life, with delightful cafés popping up in neighbourhoods everywhere. Whether you're in the mood for a sleek lounge, a funky DJ dance-bar or an oak-panelled medieval pub — read on.

42 **The Portrait Restaurant**
41 The National Portrait Gallery, St Martin's Place

The National Portrait Gallery has always been one London's must-see museums, but a recent extension and refurbishment have given it one of the best views in London. On top of the new Ondaatje wing, just behind the National Gallery on Trafalgar Square, the gallery's roof-top restaurant has magnificent views across London – the ideal place for an afternoon tea or late afternoon cocktail. With Nelson's Column rising up from a roofscape of white and verdigris domes, and Big Ben in the distance, the true drama of London's architecture is revealed in full.

42 The Drawing Room

5 Brown's Hotel, 30–34 Albemarle Street

In 1837, the year Victoria became Queen of England, James Brown, a former valet to Lord Byron, decided to open a 'top class, genteel inn', which over the years has hosted British royalty, American presidents and a fair share of celebrities. It still displays its high Victorian charms, particularly in the delightfully indulgent ritual of afternoon tea. This is the apotheosis of English tea, with finger sandwiches, warm scones, clotted cream, decadent cakes and a selection of the world's finest blends, including Brown's own Afternon Blend and 'flower infusions'.

A new take on the hotel bar, sensuously reimagined by designer David Collins, the Blue Bar takes the Regency interior to a new level of chic. Vivid blue – what Collins calls 'Lutyens blue' – and a white onyx bar and crocodile-leather print floor set the scene, with bull's-eye mirrors, Art Déco–style chairs and tasselled hanging lamps adding appropriate flourishes. Reflecting surfaces shine, as does the sparkling service. The cocktail selection, served with honeyed nuts, is civilized – no silly concoctions – mainly martinis, champagne cocktails and grown-up drinks.

Off the busy, gritty travel hub of King's Cross, on a narrow cobblestoned alley in an emerging warehouse area, Smithy's barely makes itself known, but the unassuming exterior conceals one of the capital's most atmospheric wine bars. What used to be a 19th-century horse-drawn bus garage is the setting for a huge selection of wines by the glass or bottle, with light bar meals to soak up any excess. As the area around King's Cross is seeing regeneration, so has a new owner at Smithy's tidied up a bit to ensure that the place's old character retains its charm.

DRIPPING WITH HISTORY

42 Gordon's Wine Bar

42 47 Villiers Street

If there ever was a truly down-to-earth wine bar, Gordon's is it. From 1364 it was a warehouse for cargoes of sherry and port coming off the busy river Thames. Its origins as a wine bar date from around 1870 and it has been in the hands of its current owner for more than 30 years. Today, you can still enjoy a glass of one of 80 wines in the subterranean medieval vaults that literally drip with ambience. The incomparable interiors, teeming with loyal customers (especially after work), bring alive another time that couldn't be re-created anywhere else.

CHAMPAGNE AT THE TOP

86 Vertigo[42]

5 Tower 42, 25 Old Broad Street

For security reasons, you'll need to call in advance (one day for lunch, three weeks for evening drinks) to enjoy one of the most breathtaking views of London while sipping champagne. Curvy, bright-blue, swivelling armchairs take full advantage of the vistas from the 42nd floor, atop the tallest building in the City of London. Although the bar serves mainly champagne – 30 varieties at last count – there is a selection of wines as well as oysters, lobster, caviar and sushi. You pay for the view – but it's hard to imagine a better way to do so.

60

Ye Olde Mitre Tavern

27 Ely Court, off Hatton Gardens

The Mitre's history goes back to 1546 when it was built by Bishop Goodrich for the servants of Ely Palace. The palace appears in Shakespeare's *Richard II*, Doctor Johnson is said to have visited the tavern itself, and today you can still see the trunk of a cherry tree around which Queen Elizabeth is said to have danced on May Day. Probably the most attractive pub in London – and the hardest to find – the Mitre's small rooms and dark-wood panelling retain a pub atmosphere almost impossible to find elsewhere: no music, just the pleasing din of people chatting.

86 **The Blackfriar**

2 174 Queen Victoria Street

Built on the site of a Dominican monastery that is today a rather unprepossessing concrete traffic interchange, the only Art Nouveau pub in a city dominated by Victoriana is an unexpected delight. Just across the Thames from the Tate Modern, the fantastic marble and gold-mosaiced 19th-century interior is largely overlooked, despite its curious and intimate 'grotto' (carved from a railway vault). The interior flourishes are made more appealing, perhaps, by the pub's pleasingly unprecious nature, as if it supposed all places should be like this.

THE ENGLISH BEER GARDEN

72 **The Albion**

20 10 Thornhill Road

A former coaching inn in a patrician residential neighbourhood of Islington, the delightful Albion feels like a country pub in the middle of the city. The well-heeled locals and some of the area's media crowd have ensured its reputation as a good solid old pub with wood settles and benches and cosy corners for quiet conversation. But the Albion's most exceptional feature, invisible from the front, is its enclosed, wisteria-covered back garden, which becomes a destination for people all over London during the warmer months.

SHABBY GENTILITY
28 Anglesea Arms
10 15 Selwood Terrace

Just north of the shopping highway that is the Fulham Road, the Anglesea Arms sits in quiet repose, offering a welcoming embrace with outdoor tables in leafy shadows and a discreet period air that bespeaks the days when it was presented as a gift to Lady Joseph from her husband, Sir Maxwell Joseph. This is a pub whose early Victorian charms are well preserved, along with decorative details, such as framed old photographs and historic engravings, shaded chandeliers and velvet swag draperies that provide a reliably pleasing encounter every time.

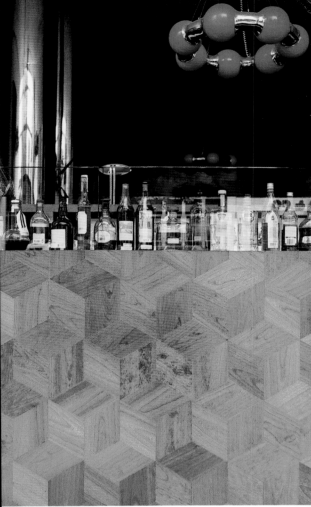

Windsor Castle

There's simply no modern way to create an interior that exudes the welcoming, gently time-worn ambience of the Windsor Castle, built in 1828, which appears to have remained virtually untouched for over two centuries. Far from feeling rarefied, the pub – once an inn – seems as though it's always been an integral part of the quiet residential area in which it's set. While the deep wood atmosphere warms in winter, a large tree-shaded garden invites pleasurable drinking in summer. A place for quiet conversation or contemplation, whatever the season.

Restaurateur Oliver Peyton has had a lot of hits over recent years, and Isola, a bar and restaurant, is one of them. Though the Italian with contemporary twists has plenty of draw, it is the ruby-red haven of handcrafted cocktails upstairs that provides the catalyst for designer drinking. Geometric-patterned wood surfaces, an overdimensioned room with a floor-to-ceiling glass wall, red leather everywhere and retro chandeliers come together in an artful combination. Your evening begins here.

'Work should be play, because play is culture, culture is networking, networking is freedom and freedom is the best condition for working in,' so do Simon and Nicholas Kirkham describe the Westbourne Studios, a creative hive where small businesses and studios come together in a formerly derelict site under the A40 motorway. A catalyst in this interaction is Under the Westway, a hip bar and restaraunt where people from the studios and the public can mingle, network, hang out or see one of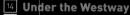

Just off Old Street, Dragon Bar suggests its artistic origins and insider inclinations in details like the boxy concrete portico with discreet lettering on the bottom step and graffiti-splattered lavatories. Inside, a house DJ spins a rock-funky mix, sofas and chairs are strewn around seemingly at random. Against the sea of bars for the after-work crowd that are encroaching on Shoreditch's creative vibe, the Dragon is resolutely bohemian ('no office clothes'). For some this requires a leap of faith; for others, this is, and has been, the real

Named after the brothels that were once sought out by sailors in port, not completely without meaning in this area of King's Cross, the Ruby Lounge has accomplished the somewhat contradictory task of making a rundown area more inviting. Along the ramshackle collection of improving and crumbling shopfronts, the Ruby Lounge's glowing red logo outside and breathtaking Vernon Panton chandelier and wall lights inside are welcome signs in the night. The music is groovy, as are the people.

From its origins as a migrating Sunday afternoon dance club to one of the happiest venues in the West End, The Social is a product of the Heavenly record and club producers, whose parties have seen some of London's most famous DJs. In 1999, David Adjaye, architect of choice for London's Brit Artists, remodelled the interiors using unconventional exterior materials to create a two-level space that allows for all variety of dance activity but is difficult to characterize. Add to that exceptionally clued-in music and a happy crowd, and you've found your haven.

Under the arches of the Kingsland Viaduct, Cargo has taken on an ambitious task of providing restaurant, bar and club venue all under a series of vaulted roofs and making them all seem very cool. With vague dockside theme, the branded Cargo logo greets you but that is the only given here. The open dining area is filled with giant square wood tables and views out to the planted courtyard garden. Music is one of the principal draws here, with regular performances and internationally renowned DJs making the scene.

Downstairs from the Red Fort (p.142), and in the same spirit of creating a complete experience, Akbar's interior resembles a lavish palace lounge, with a caverned seating area and plenty of cushions and tassels along with a suitably exotic and original cocktail list. Arrive early for dinner and indulge in a Great Mughal, a raisin-infused Woodford Reserve bourbon, passionfruit juice, lime and lemongrass cordial and rosewater; or arrive later to enjoy the Asian-influenced dance vibe.

Hoxton Square

In the last five or so years, Hoxton Square has become synonymous with hip studio during the daytime and groovy bars at night, largely supplanting Soho as a night-time destination. Inevitably, with the discovery of the area, many of the creatives who made the area what it is have moved on – but the vibe, day and night, remains intact, if made up more than visitors and locals. Interestingly, most of the places that formed the early night life are still there, and still draw a crowd. Slightly off the square, a large, minimally furnished space with plate

glass windows, aglow with neon, announces what used to be electricity showrooms but has been for the last several years one of the area's principal watering holes. With a prominent but not prepossessing position on the southwest corner of Hoxton Square is Bluu, formerly the Blue Note club, which many would argue was the epicenter of drum 'n' bass dance music. Five years later it features a modern stainless-steel-trimmed interior and DJs who continue the tradition of its predecessor. Next door and down one level, this time lacking in signage, is the Hoxton Square Bar and Kitchen, another of the area's standbys. The open interior, set slightly below ground level, is animated at night by the eerie sensation of car headlights, as they turn just before the bar. A few blocks away is Liquid, a small but vividly coloured venue that comes alive at night. Heading somewhat south to Great Eastern Street are Medicine Bar, a fairly recent arrival, and the Great Eastern Dining Rooms, which in addition to its bar and downstairs lounge serves respectable Italian food.

shop

Like most metropolises, London is a hive of commercial activity, buzzing with grand department stores, stylish international-label outlets and off-beat boutiques. At the other end of the style spectrum are the dozens of street markets where real Londoners sell everything from antiques to country produce. Energized by the capital's renowned design schools, boutiques and speciality shops are springing up around the city – but are often off the beaten track. To understand what London style is all about, you need to seek the individualists who keep London on the global fashion map. For classic British labels or unheard-of street-chic upstarts, here is a guide.

Since she made her first collection of brocade mules in 1985, Emma Hope has won a number of design awards, including several from the Design Council, as well as one from *Harper's and Queen*. It is not hard to see why her lovingly detailed shoes should have garnered so much praise. Apart from fine leathers, Emma Hope shoes are made in such luxurious materials as nappa, suede, silk velvet, embroidered brocade and grosgrain, all designed by her and fabricated in Florence. Elegant and craftsmanlike, Hope has expanded her range to complementary bags.

A Cornish farmboy who learned the bootmaking craft, John Lobb received a royal warrant for his work from Edward, Prince of Wales, later Edward VII. Today the company holds three royal warrants from the Queen, the Duke of Edinburgh and the current Prince of Wales. The shop is a shrine to craftsmanship, as John Lobb still specialize in and have become almost synonymous with the art of the hand-made shoe. Each pair is numbered and fitted with its own shoe trees. Buckskin, satin calf and ostrich are just some of the leathers available.

Manolo Blahnik's gold-accented shop is a must-see for any lover of footwear, with dramatic displays that raise shoes to the level of art objects, and many are just that, as his customers around the world are fully aware – Madonna says they're 'better than sex'. There is a high degree of concept, design and craftsmanship behind each pair of 'Manolos', the last for which the Canary Islands–born designer carves himself. Leathers are dyed in bright contrasting colours like pink and yellow or turquoise and lime. Despite his now firmly established fame, since first being 'discovered' by legendary fashion editor Diana Vreeland in 1970 and more recently brought into public consciousness by *Sex and the City*, Blahnik is still the perfectionist who controls every aspect of the design and manufacture, and his first store in Chelsea is the place to find the genuine article.

Starting out as a gopher in a clothing warehouse at 18, Paul Smith has gone on to become probably England's best-known menswear designer. Though he still has a solid reputation for cool elegance in men's fashion, particularly in Japan, in England his presence is comparatively slight. Since branching into women's and children's wear and home fashion, his original shop in Covent Garden (p. 54) has been somewhat superseded by the design emporium at Westbourne House in Notting Hill. Living the designer's dream, Smith obtained a large, double-fronted Victorian corner house and filled it with his personal vision, which consists of the full range of his clothing and home ware, as well as his first bespoke tailoring service. Paul Smith may be widely available, but the Westbourne House experience feels like a glimpse into his private world.

The most famous street for men's suits in the world needs no introduction, but times have changed, and the prevailing trend to modernize classics is influencing the look on Savile Row. Led by innovators such as Ozwald Boetang (p. 171), a generation of ever-so-slightly daring or even irreverent younger tailors are beginning to seize control. Amid the highly traditional shops are edgier talents, such as Richard James, who has been honoured by the British Fashion Council and has attracted a younger clientele with his modern cuts and banned advertisements. The Duffer of St George provides classic cuts with vivid colours and has spawned a veritable subculture in the street. For a glimpse back in time, peek into the timeless office of age-old Anderson & Sheppard, who are perhaps best known for dressing royalty and where British fashion star Alexander McQueen cut his cloth as a teenager. William Hunt's sartorial flair has won him a number of music-world clients.

42 **Agent Provocateur**

39 6 Broadwick Street

In late 1994 Joseph Corre and Serena Rees created a stir with the opening of their first lingerie shop. 'Adult entertainment' is a generic statement of their unique talent for titillation, but their continued popularity owes more to their commitment to projecting an image of 'positive sexuality'. Combining eroticism and humour with fine quality and an emphasis on glamour, Agent Provocateur has been wildly successful. The shop is an experience in sensual pleasures with a 'boudoir-style' interior and shop assistants in high heels, lace stockings and bustiers designed by Vivienne Westwood.

14 **Dinny Hall**

16 200 Westbourne Grove

Despite the appearance of her pieces in the fashion press and the roster of high-profile clients, there is something pleasingly understated about Dinny Hall jewelry. The lines are simple and the cuts of precious and semiprecious stones correspondingly elegant. Hall's status as a top British designer was confirmed when she was commissioned to design a line for the new Tate Modern when it opened in 2000. The jewelry is handmade in the studio just behind the Westbourne Grove shop, and the prices are almost ridiculously reasonable given her universal appeal and demand.

Irishman Philip Treacy's approach to millinery is that of a sculptor. He staged the first catwalk show of his own designs in 1993 with the help of supermodels Christy Turlington, Kate Moss and Naomi Campbell. But Treacy's designs are worth the attention on their own, whether it's a pale pink top hat set off with a giant silk rose, a proliferation of green leaves sprouting from a headband or a delicate swirl perched atop a well-groomed forehead. And while he designs for some of the most exclusive customers, he also makes a not-so-haute range, available in this shop, that lesser mortals can enjoy.

Westbourne Grove is chock-a-block with designer boutiques, but this gem of a bespoke jewelry shop is slightly removed from the fray. Despite the ruby-red front, it doesn't announce itself, and though you are welcome to drop in, you must make an appointment if you want a consultation with the lady herself. Having worked for costume jewellers Butler & Wilson (see p. 32), Azagury-Partridge is one of Britain's most inventive jewelry designers, whose bold, baroque creations in 18k yellow, white and rose gold and platinum are full of shape, colour and wit.

42 Selfridges

19 400 Oxford Street

Up until very recently, Selfridges was a massive store with an impressive block-long façade housing a rambling not particularly impressive set of predictable concessions, the whole of which seems imperilled by the new fashion labels and their ever sexier flagship stores. Enter Vittorio Radice in 1996, whose experience as international buyer at Habitat put him in touch with a design-savvy public hungry for novel retail environments. Radice revivified the ailing giant, reinvented a number of departments, refurbished the entire store and brought in new labels,

talent, look and vibe. And now Selfridges is hot. Although still essentially a store of brands – over 3000 at last count – it has gone a long way to promote young, home-grown talent (in its Design Lab section), while providing a majestic setting for known brands. The men's department features leading-edge Savile Row tailors and established English brands; while everything imaginable is on sale for women. The children's section, too, has unexpected (if pricey) articles. The basement features a number of concessions carrying off-beat furniture and domestic objects. Even for the jaded global-brand hunter, Selfridges redefines 'one-stop' shopping for a new, discerning generation of consumers. If you've only got two hours to shop in London, make this your first destination.

The street of men's shirtmakers is a must-see for anyone looking to procure the genuine English article, from shoes to shirts. Harvie and Hudson, which was founded in 1929, is at no. 97, and even if their traditional style is not to your liking, the fine Victorian shopfront is worth the short walk from any of the numerous establishments. Dunhill, now available worldwide, started out as Alfred Dunhill the tobacconist before becoming the global purveyor of fine menswear and accessories, today with a decidedly modern edge. Provisions of a different sort are available at J. Floris, the oldest perfumer in London, established as a barber shop in 1730 by Juan Famenias Floris of Menorca. The shop's interior is bejewelled with the bottled essences, candles, soaps and lotions, some displayed in the Spanish mahogany cabinets that were obtained from the Great Exhibition of 1852. For shirts, it must be Turnbull & Asser, probably the street's best-known shop, which also features bespoke shirts. Fine mother-of-pearl buttons, specially woven Sea Island cotton, 'the most gentlemanly of shirtings', and broad, three-buttoned cuffs are among Turnbull & Asser's trademarks.

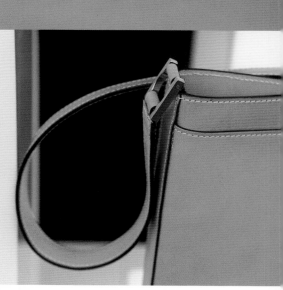

If you love leather the way Bill Amberg loves leather then you will love just about everything he does. His affinity for the stuff means that he doesn't make dainty strappy accessories but things that you can run your hand over, smell or walk on. From cowhide leather floors to vellum for a drawer liner, he expertly works each kind to its advantage. His women's bags are ample and luxuriously free of fussy details, as are his men's modern but supple cases and accessories. Attention is given to shape and to the smooth finish, texture and deep colours.

One of Britain's oldest leather-goods stores, frequented for generations by royalty and the well-heeled alike, Tanner Krolle – like so many British labels – has recently had a facelift. After centuries of creating 'the finest English bridle leather pieces without compromise in respect to either craft or materials', the small firm's Burlington Gardens store continues to pride itself on producing goods of the highest quality while giving their purses, handbags and luggage (including laptop cases) a contemporary edge that has attracted a new generation of devotees.

42 **Connolly**

4 41 Conduit Street

Until 2000 Connolly was known principally as the exquisite upholstery of choice for Rolls Royces, Jaguars, Astin Martins and Ferraris. Since then, the company has expanded to include a wide range of leather goods, from log books to carrying cases, as well as clothing (designed by Joseph Ettedgui) and shoes (by Tim Little) and an Andrée Putman–designed store in the heart of Mayfair. Their leather goods, which include attaché-case ranges designed by Seymore Powell and Ross Lovegrove, are the best money can buy.

BESPOKE MASTERY

42 **Ozwald Boateng**

20 9 Vigo Street

No one in recent years has caused a stir in 'traditional' men's fashion quite like Ozwald Boateng. Taking his cue from classic British men's suits, Boateng has injected a certain exoticism and a flair for cut and colour that have utterly transformed the quintessential jacket and trousers while retaining their integrity. Tones, patterns and fabrics that might have once been sniffed at have attained new levels of acceptability in Boateng's 'bespoke couture' collection. His suits are among the most sought-after in London – for those well-dressed who dare to be different.

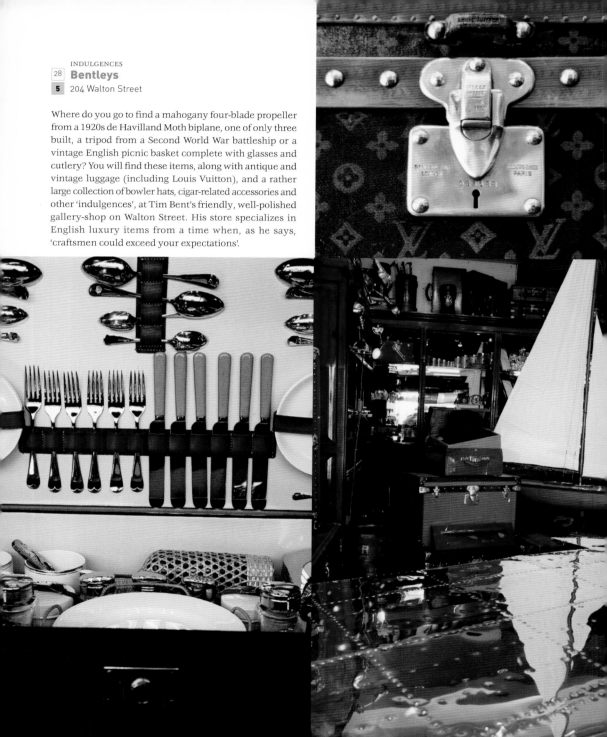

Where do you go to find a mahogany four-blade propeller from a 1920s de Havilland Moth biplane, one of only three built, a tripod from a Second World War battleship or a vintage English picnic basket complete with glasses and cutlery? You will find these items, along with antique and vintage luggage (including Louis Vuitton), and a rather large collection of bowler hats, cigar-related accessories and other 'indulgences', at Tim Bent's friendly, well-polished gallery-shop on Walton Street. His store specializes in English luxury items from a time when, as he says, 'craftsmen could exceed your expectations'.

David Mellor operates on the simple principle that well-designed equipment can improve your life. Mellor, Royal Designer for Industry, has an international reputation as designer, manufacturer and shopkeeper. Born in Sheffield, he has always specialized in metalwork and has often been described as 'the cutlery king'. Mellor opened his Sloane Square shop in 1969. Today it sells his own range of tableware and a large selection of kitchen accessories. Mellor trained as a silversmith and is known for his own cutlery range, which he began designing in the 1950s and which is available in silver plate and stainless steel, all manufactured in England. While some of his pieces are based on historic British designs, all have a classic, modern shape. His kitchenware items – pans and grills, kitchen tools and knives, coffee machines and pasta makers – are sourced from specialist factories in Europe. The shop also carries fine table pottery and glass that are exclusive to the David Mellor shops. His collection also features his first range of professional kitchen knives in high-grade stainless steel, which exploit the latest technological advances to achieve their unique sculptural form.

60 **Gallery 1930/Susie Cooper Ceramics**

2 18 Church Street

Probably London's most comprehensive collection of Art Déco ceramics, furniture and lighting is housed in a small but richly filled shop on a road that is like a secret hoard of antiques dealers. Alfie's, a collection of dealers' stalls, has been going for years. Geoffrey Peake and Nick Jones first set up shop at Alfie's as Susie Cooper Ceramics, selling mostly the work of the 'quintessentially English designer', who began working in the 1920s. They have relocated to their own premises and offer a wide collection of boldy patterned Clarice Cliff vessels and solid-hued Keith Murray designs for Wedgwood.

VINTAGE STREET

14 **Rellik**

19 8 Golborne Road

Located in edgy Ladbroke Grove opposite Myro Goldfinger's brutalist triumph (or terror, some might say), Trellik Tower, Rellik is a second-hand shop with a difference, as its loyal customers and fashion-magazine editors are well aware. Three former Portobello Road stall owners set up shop to offer select vintage wear from the 1920s onward, each with her own area of speciality, including both ready-to-wear and couture pieces. If you look hard enough, you might just find a classic Westwood outfit.

DREAMY DRAPERY
14 **Ghost**

26 36 Ledbury Road

Tanya Sarne's drapey, dreamy creations have been accumulating applause and fashion awards since 1990. Designed, as she says, 'by women for women', they are intended to make every woman feel beautiful. Sarne eschews hard lines, concentrating instead on 'how a fabric feels against the skin'. To that end, her vintage crepe, velvet and satin, for example, are put through a special production process to achieve their sensuous flowing quality. The shop in Ledbury Road is her flagship store, which reflects her unique blend of relaxed femininity.

NECESSARY ACCESSORIES
28 **Anya Hindmarch**

21 15–17 Pont Street

Anya Hindmarch found her style niche at the age of 19, when she discovered the fondness Italian women had for simple drawstring bags. Her designs are colourful, witty and well-crafted: photo-print beach scenes look like vintage postcards and beaded mosaic pop-art bags, such as the 'Heinz Baked Beans' bag with a beaded 'label' stiched on to a tin-shaped denim carrier, have become classics. In 2002 she launched a shoe collection, for which she produced green pumps and a matching bag featuring a striking reproduction of a Rose's Lime Juice label.

retreat

It is probably true that the real England is in the country, not in the cities. And though the regions immediately surrounding London's concrete jungle are in many ways bucolic translations of the city sensibility, it is not hard to find pockets — by the sea, in the countryside, in villages — that feel worlds away, even though some are a mere 30 minutes by train from the city. These four getaways represent very different experiences, but each is distinctly English and an ideal tonic after an intoxicating few days in the urban buzz.

Brighton: Seaside Hip
- Blanch House
- Hotel Pelirocco

Formerly the playground of Regency royals and today a hip seaside clubbing destination, Brighton is the quintessential English getaway, particularly for the youthfully inclined. Dynamized by students from the local university, one of the liveliest nightclub scenes in the the the U.K., if not Europe, the recreation destination is just over an hour from London. An unusually high concentration of record and jewelry shops, quarters of narrow pedestrianized lanes and the wide-open boardwalk unite in a cool concoction of kitsch, fun, craft and decadence.

The town centre has four principal quarters: North Laine, a tight grid of quaint, brightly coloured houses with lively boutiques and bars; the Lanes, a rabbit warren of even narrower alleyways packed with clothes shops and jewellers; the Seafront, which features a boardwalk and the Arches, a long colonnade comprising mainly restaurants and bars, many of which turn into nightclubs when day becomes night; and Kemp Town, east of the pier, between St James Street and Marina Drive, with a more relaxed vibe.

At opposite ends of the action, are two hotels whose character fits perfectly with the Brighton scene. Blanch House, a delightful 12-room hotel opened in 2001 by Amanda Blanch and Chris Edwardes in Kemp Town, is intimate, with each room quirkily themed and cleverly decorated; its small restaurant serves contemporary British. Hotel Pelirocco, on Regency Square, is all rock 'n' roll (without the volume): Playstations in every room, idiosyncratic decoration and a host of guests from London's hip music scene have garnered the hotel international attention and a colourful following.

For a relatively small town, there is a high concentration of shops, over 300 at last count, many of which are independently owned and feature a broad spectrum of wares, from streetwear and locally designed crafts to 1970s furniture and decorative objects, to kites and beachwear – with prices generally noticeably lower than their London counterparts. One must not miss the Royal Pavilion, a faux-exotic pleasure palace built by George IV in 1785 as a residence – an entirely appropriate symbol of the town's exuberance and excess.

Bath and Babington House:
Georgian Splendour, Contemporary Style
Somerset

Londoners have been going to Bath for rest and rejuvenation probably since the Romans first exploited the natural hot springs. But it was at the height of popularity as a retreat for the fashionable rich during the 18th century, when English architects John Wood and son created the elegant neo-Classical squares and crescents using golden Bath stone, making it one of the most picturesque cities in England – today just over an hour by train from London. The city's heart is the convergence of the Abbey Church (1616), the Roman Baths and Museum and the Pump Room, a grand 18th-century tea-room that gives something of the flavour of Bath society popularized by Jane Austen. In the elevated northwest near the park and botanic gardens, the Royal Crescent is a masterpiece of 18th-century architecture.

Restaurants and lodgings are abundant in Bath but a stylish and fitting base is just a few miles away, near Frome, in the early Georgian country estate of Babington House where 18th-century charm and modern convenience have been married to fruitful success. Nick Jones, the enterprising figure behind the Soho Club and the refurbished Electric Cinema (p. 23) in London, has brought modern comforts – such as a heated outdoor swimming pool, a cinema, clubby bar (try the house champagne cocktail or hot toddy) and gourmet restaurant – to a discerning urban crowd and nestled them comfortably in the arms of this grand country house. Drawing rooms with furniture by contemporary designers and rustic-chic room décor that respect the architecture have transformed the manor house into a very singular environment. With gym and spa facilities housed in a former cowshed, which overlooks the two lap pools, the picture is complete. Everything is perfectly in keeping with Bath's history as a place of high fashion: there is nothing that Georgian aristocrats wouldn't expect to find here, were they cavorting here in the 21st century. The large light-filled breakfast room offers meals almost any time of day and the restaurant delivers high-quality dishes that take full advantage of local and organic produce.

Bray: an Epicurean Destination

- The Fat Duck
- The Waterside Inn
- Monkey Island Hotel

A mere 30-minute train journey from Paddington station takes you to what must be the highest concentration of Michelin stars in the country, set in the verdant Thames-side setting of Bray, a 16th-century village. Just a few minutes apart, The Waterside Inn and The Fat Duck, both in converted country pubs, have set the very highest standards in culinary excellence – in completely different ways.

The Waterside Inn was opened by Albert and Michel Roux, the brothers who in 1967 redefined London's world of gastronomy with the opening of Le Gavroche, still one of the city's premier classic French restaurants. Today Michel and his son Alain, who has recently assumed the helm, to rave reviews, run the Waterside Inn with the élan and elegance that have made its modern classic French cuisine an institution. Despite the excellence of the food and service, the converted pub surroundings and dining room overlooking the river impart a notably unstuffy air – formality softened and democratized by countryside.

A newer arrival, and pursuing excellence in a very different manner, The Fat Duck is the product of Heston Blumenthal. Since opening the restaurant in 1995, he has explored innovative modes of cooking that draw on science rather than relying on conventional kitchen methods. His intensive research into chemistry, psychology and sensory perception – an approach sometimes referred to as 'molecular gastronomy' – has uncovered an entire spectrum of tastes, moods and memories that he believes could be the first revolution in cooking since nouvelle cuisine. In the recently remodelled interior with an intimate 45 seats, the results are startling and exciting.

After such splendid dining experiences, you will want nothing more than to fall asleep to the sound of the Thames lapping against its banks. For those too sated to move, the Waterside Inn offers 10 rooms in the main house and outbuildings around the site. On a tiny Thames island close to both restaurants, the peaceful Monkey Island Hotel is a historical property accessed only by a pedestrian bridge. Most of its 26 rooms have river or garden views.

THE WATERSIDE

ELIZABETHAN BOLT-HOLE

Gravetye Manor: the Ultimate Country House Experience

East Grinstead, West Sussex

Less than 30 miles southwest of London, a thousand acres of forest are the setting for one of the southeast's most luxurious country-house hotels. After a 50-minute train ride from central London you arrive in the Sussex town of East Grinstead; a short taxi drive takes you through green countryside to historic Gravetye Manor. Built in 1598 by Richard Infield for his wife, Katherine, the stone mansion retains most of its Elizabethan elements, despite periods of neglect. Some of the windows are still ornamented with delicate wrought-iron glazing bars and open to the expanse of gardens and fields that were tamed and encouraged by a renowned English landscape gardener, William Robinson.

Robinson bought the manor and the surrounding land in 1884 and lived there until he died in 1935, laying out the gardens of small plants and flowers, trees and shrubs, and pioneering what became known as the English 'natural' style. The arrangement of the gardens is his living legacy and no small part of the appeal of Gravetye, which was bought by Peter Herbert and converted to a hotel in 1958.

The interiors are enchanting. Warm wood rooms, printed English fabrics, period portraits and flowers, as well as service that is informal but highly discreet and attentive, make guests feel truly welcome in an atmosphere of old-world luxury. Two wood-panelled drawing rooms, each with a well-tended wood fire, can be used by guests for quiet reading, relaxing or for having tea or drinks. The restaurant, led by chef Mark Raffan, has earned a Michelin star, so requires booking ahead. Around lunch you might consider a walk through the countryside to the rustic pub of a neighbouring village.

Rooms are finely decorated in traditional English style, even with the occasional ceiling or floor slant that is so much part of the character of this cherished old property. Peter and Susan Herbert strive to maintain an air that is 'not trendy but at the same time not aged and stuffy'. Their 40 years of experience with the house and the clientele ensure that their delightful establishment will continue for many years.

contact

All telephone numbers are given for dialling locally: the country code for England is 44; the city code for London 20. Calling from abroad, therefore, one dials (+44 20) plus the number given below. Telephone numbers in the retreat section are given for dialling from London: if calling from abroad, dial the country code (44) and drop the 0 at the start of the number. The number in brackets by the name is the page number on which the entry appears.

Adam Street [142]
8 Adam Street
London WC2N 6AA
T   7379 8000
F   7379 1444
E   reception@adamstreet.co.uk
W   www.adamstreet.co.uk

The Admiralty [57]
Somerset House
The Strand
London WC2R 1LA
T   7845 4646
W   www.somerset-house.org.uk

After Noah [80]
121 Upper Street
London N1 1QP
T F 7359 4281
W   www.afternoah.com

Agent Provocateur [166]
6 Broadwick Street
London W1V 1FH
T   7439 0229
F   7287 3795
W   www.agentprovocateur.com

Akbar [158]
(Beneath Red Fort)
77 Dean Street
London W1D 3SH
T   7437 2525
F   7434 0721
E   info@redfort.co.uk
W   www.redfort.co.uk/akbar

The Albion [153]
10 Thornhill Road
London N1 1HW
T   7607 7450

Alfred [66]
245 Shaftesbury Avenue
London WC2H 8EH
T   7240 2566
F   7497 0672

Almeida Theatre [83]
Almeida Street
London N1 1TA
T · 7226 7432
W   www.almeida.co.uk

Anderson & Sheppard Ltd [165]
30 Savile Row
London W1S 3PT
T   7734 1420
F   7734 1721
E   office@anderson-sheppard.co.uk

Anglesea Arms [154]
15 Selwood Terrace
London SW7 3QG
T   7373 7960

Annie's [83]
12 Camden Passage
London N1 8ED
T   7359 0796
F   7359 2116

Antoni & Alison [74]
Factory of Lights and Experiment
43 Rosebery Avenue
London EC1R 4SH
T F 7833 2002
E   info@antoniandalison.co.uk
W   www.antoniandalison.co.uk

Anya Hindmarch [175]
15–17 Pont Street
London SW1X 9EH
T   7838 9177

F   7838 9111
W   www.anyahindmarch.com

Anything Left-Handed [49]
57 Brewer Street
London W1F 9UL
T   7437 3910
W   www.anythingleft-handed.co.uk

Applied Arts Agency [76]
30 Exmouth Market
London EC1R 4QE
T   7837 2632
E   appliedartsagency@lineout.net

aQuaint [57]
38 Monmouth Street
London WC2H 9EP
T   7240 9677
F   7240 4209

@Work [90]
156 Brick Lane
London E1 6RU
T F 7377 0597
W   www.atworkgallery.com

The Avenue [135]
7–9 St James's Street
London SW1A 1EE
T   7321 2111
F   7321 2500
E   avenue@egami.co.uk
W   www.theavenue.co.uk

Baby Ceylon [23]
Unit 16, Portobello Green Arcade
281 Portobello Road
London W10 5TZ
T   8968 9501

Baltic [105]
74 Blackfriars Road
London SE1 8HA
T   7928 1111
F   7928 8487
E   info@balticrestaurant.co.uk
W   www.balticrestaurant.co.uk

Bare [64]
8 Chiltern Street
London W1U 7PU
T   7486 7779
E   daisymorrison@hotmail.com

Basia Zarzycka [34]
52 Sloane Square
London SW1W 8AX
T   7730 1660
F   7730 0065
E   graham@basias.com
W   www.basias.com

Bed Bar [20]
310 Portobello Road
London W10 5TA
T   8969 4500

Bentleys [172]
204 Walton Street
London SW3 2JL
T   7584 7770
F   7584 8182
E   shop@bentleyslondon.com
W   www.bentleyslondon.com

Bermondsey Market [101]
Bermondsey Square
London SE1

Bibendum Oyster Bar [31]
Michelin House
81 Fulham Road

London SW3 6RD
T 7589 1480
F 7823 7925
E manager@bibendum.co.uk

Bill Amberg [170]
10 Chepstow Road
London W10 5NT
T 7727 3560
F 7727 3541
W www.billamberg.com

The Blackfriar [153]
174 Queen Victoria Street
London EC4B 4EG
T 7236 5474

Blenheim Books [24]
11 Blenheim Crescent
London W11 2EE
T 7792 0777
E sales@blenheimbooks.co.uk

Blue Bar [150]
The Berkeley Hotel
Wilton Place
London SW1X 7RL
T 7201 1680
F 7235 4330
E ncowan@the-berkeley.co.uk
W www.the-berkeley.co.uk

Bluu Bar [159]
1 Hoxton Square
London N1 6NU
T 7613 2793

Boiler House [90]
Brick Lane, opposite Truman Brewery
London E1

bookartbookshop [92]
17 Pitfield Street
London N1 6HB
T 7608 1333
W www.bookartbookshop.com

Boxfresh [57]
2 Shorts Gardens
London WC2 9AU
T 7240 4742
W www.boxfresh.co.uk

Boyd [37]
42 Elizabeth Street
London SW1W 9NZ
T 7730 3939
F 7730 3535

Brick Lane Beigel Bake [90]
159 Brick Lane
London E1 6TS
T 7729 0616

Bridge and Tunnel [89]
4 Calvert Avenue
London E2 7JP
T 7729 6533
E info@bridgeandtunnel.co.uk
W www.bridgeandtunnel.co.uk

Brown's Hotel [149]
30–34 Albemarle Street
London W1S 4BP
T 7493 6020
F 7493 9381
W www.brownshotel.com

Browns + Browns Focus [44]
Browns: 23–27 South Molton Street
London W1K 5RD
Browns Focus: 38–39 South Molton
Street

London W1K 5RN
T 7514 0000
F 7408 1281
W www.brownsfashion.com

Bruce Oldfield [32]
27 Beauchamp Place
London SW3 1NJ
T 7584 1363

Burlington Arcade (off Piccadilly) [48]
Royal Arcade (off Bond Street)
London W1
W www.burlington-arcade.co.uk

Burro [54]
29 Floral Street
London WC2 E9DP
T 7240 5120
F 7379 7465
E sales@burro.co.uk
W www.burro.co.uk

Butler & Wilson [32]
189 Fulham Road
London SW3 6JN
T 7352 3045
F 7376 5981
E info@butlerandwilson.co.uk
W www.butlerandwilson.com

Butlers Wharf Chop House [102]
The Butlers Wharf Building
36e Shad Thames
London SE1 2YE
T 7403 3403
F 7403 3414
W www.conran-restaurants.co.uk

C2+ [75]
33 Clerkenwell Green
London EC1R 0DU
T 7251 9200
F 7251 5655
E c2@lesleycrazegallery.co.uk

Café 1001 [91]
Dray Walk
Brick Lane
London E1

Canal [80]
42 Cross Street
London N1 2BA
T 7704 0222

Cantina del Ponte [102]
The Butlers Wharf Building
36c Shad Thames
London SE1 2YE
T 7403 5403
F 7403 4432
W www.conran-restaurants.co.uk

Carhartt [51]
13 Newburgh Street
London W1
T 7287 6411
W www.thecarharttstore.co.uk

Cargo [158]
83 Rivington Street
London EC2A 3AY
T 7739 3440
F 7739 3441
W www.cargo-london.com

Cath Kidston [17]
8 Clarendon Cross
London W11 4AP
T 7221 4000

F 7229 1992
W www.cathkidston.co.uk

Chelsea Physic Garden [32]
66 Royal Hospital Road
London SW3 4HS
T 7352 5646
F 7376 3910
E maureen@cpgarden.demon.co.uk
W www.chelseaphysicgarden.co.uk

Christ Church Spitalfields [93]
Commercial Street
London E1 6QE
T 7247 0165

Cigala [68]
54 Lamb's Conduit Street
London WC1N 3LW
T 7405 1717
E tasty@cigala.co.uk
W www.cigala.co.uk

Cinch [51]
5 Newburgh Street
London W1V 1LH
T 7287 4941
F 7287 6496
W www.cinch-icon.co.uk

Cinnamon Club [139]
30 Great Smith Street
London SW1P 3BU
T 7222 2555
F 7222 1333
E info@cinnamonclub.com
W www.cinnamonclub.com

Circus [50]
1 Upper James Street
London W1F 9DF
T 7534 4000
F 7534 4010
E circus@egami.co.uk
W www.circusbar.co.uk

Claridge's [137]
55 Brook Street
London W1A 2JQ
T 7629 8860
F 7499 2210
E info@claridges.co.uk
W www.claridges.co.uk

Coco de Mer [57]
23 Monmouth Street
London WC2H 9DD
T 7836 8882
F 7836 8881
W www.coco-de-mer.co.uk

Comfort & Joy [80]
109 Essex Road
London N1 2FL
T 7359 3898

Connolly [171]
41 Conduit Street
London W1R 9FB
T 7439 2510
F 7439 2513

Contemporary Applied Arts [68]
2 Percy Street
London W1T 1DD
T 7436 2344
F 7436 2446
W www.caa.org.uk

Couverture [31]
310 Kings Road
London SW3 5UH
T 7795 1200

F 7795 1202
E info@couverture.co.uk
W www.couverture.co.uk

The Cow Dining Room [138]
89 Westbourne Park Road
London W2 5QH
T 7221 5400

Crafts Council [79]
44a Pentonville Road
London N1 9BY
T 7278 7700
F 7837 6891
W www.craftscouncil.org.uk

The Cross [18]
141 Portland Road
London W11 4LR
T 7727 6760
F 7727 6745

Cross Street Gallery [80]
40 Cross Street
London N1 2BA
T 7226 8600

The Crown [79]
116 Cloudesley Road
London N1 0EB
T 7837 7107
F 7833 1084
E crown.islington@fullers.co.uk

CVO Firevault [63]
36 Great Titchfield Street
London W1W 8BQ
T 7580 5333
F 7255 2234
E enquiries@cvofirevault.co.uk
W www.cvo.co.uk

Daunt Books [63]
83–84 Marylebone High Street
London W1U 4QW
T 7224 2295

David Mellor [172]
4 Sloane Square
London SW1W 8EE
T 7730 4259
F 7730 7240
W www.davidmellordesign.com

Delfina [104]
50 Bermondsey Street
London SE1 3UD
T 7357 0244
F 7357 0250
E events@delfina.org.uk
W www.delfina.org.uk

Dennis Severs's House [94]
18 Folgate Street
London E1 6BX
T 7247 4013
F 7377 5548
E info@dennissevershouse.co.uk
W www.dennissevershouse.co.uk

Design Mueseum [102]
28 Shad Thames
London SE1 2YD
T 7940 8790
F 7378 6540
W www.designmuseum.org

Designers' Guild [32]
267 and 277 King's Road
London SW3 5EN
T 7351 5775
F 7243 7710
W www.designersguild.com

Dinny Hall [166]
200 Westbourne Grove
London W11 2RH
T   7792 3913
F   7792 8322
E   sales@dinnyhall.co.uk
W   www.dinnyhall.com

The Dispensary [51]
9 Newburgh Street (womenswear)
London W1F 7RL
T   7287 8145
15 Newburgh Street (menswear)
London W1F 7RX
T   7734 4095
E   info@thedispensary.net
W   www.thedispensary.net

Donmar Warehouse [54]
41 Earlham Street
London WC2H 9LX
T   7369 1732
W   www.donmar-warehouse.co.uk

Dover Castle [64]
43 Weymouth Mews
London W1G 7EQ
T   7580 4412

Dower & Hall [32]
60 Beauchamp Place
London SW3 1NZ
T   7589 8474
F   7589 8491
W   www.dowerandhall.co.uk

Dragon Bar [156]
5 Leonard Street
London EC2A 4AQ
T   7490 7110

Dream Bags Jaguar Shoes [89]
34–36 Kingsland Road
London E2 8DA
E   carbon.industries@virgin.net

Duchamp [24]
75 Ledbury Road
London W11 2AG
T   7243 3970
F   7243 4708
E   admin@duchamp.co.uk
W   www.duchamp.co.uk

Duffer of St George [165]
31–32 Savile Row
London W1C 3PX
T   7734 3666
E   info@thedufferofstgeorge.com
W   www.thedufferofstgeorge.com

Duke of Cambridge [79]
30 St Peters Street
London N1 8JT
T   7359 3066
W   www.singhboulton.co.uk/duke

The Duke of York [66]
7 Roger Street
London WC1N 2PB
T   7242 7230

Dunhill [169]
48 Jermyn Street
London SW1Y 6DL
T   7290 8602
W   www.dunhill.com

The Eagle [138]
159 Farringdon Road
London EC1R 3AL

Eatmyhandbgbitch [91]
6 Dray Walk
The Old Truman Brewery
91–95 Brick Lane
London E1 6QL
T   7375 3100
F   7375 0959
E   contact@eatmyhandbagbitch.co.uk
W   www.eatmyhandbagbitch.co.uk

EC One [76]
41 Exmouth Market
London EC1R 4QL
T   7713 6185
F   7833 3151
W   www.econe.co.uk

Edible [76]
60 Exmouth Market
London EC1R 4QE
T   7837 0409
T   7837 0408
E   info@edible.com
W   www.edible.com

Egg [35]
36 Kinnerton Street
London SW1X 8EF
T   7235 9315
F   7838 9705
E   egg@eggtrading.com

The Electric Cinema [23]
191 Portobello Road
London W11 2ED
T   7908 9696
F   7908 9595
W   www.electriccinema.co.uk

Electricity Showrooms [159]
39a Hoxton Square
London N1 6NU
T   7739 6934
F   7739 6451
W   www.electricityshowrooms.co.uk

Eleven Cadogan Gardens [124]
11 Cadogan Gardens
London SW3 2RJ
T   7730 7000
F   7730 5217
E   reservations@
    number-eleven.co.uk
W   www.number-eleven.co.uk

Elspeth Gibson [37]
7 Pont Street
London SW1X 9EJ
T   7235 0601
F   7235 0602
W   www.elspethgibson.com

Emma Hope [162]
207 Westbourne Grove
London W11 2SE
T   7313 7490
F   7313 7491
W   www.emmahope.co.uk

The Enterprise [34]
35 Walton Street
London SW3 2HU
T   7584 3148
F   7584 2516
E   enterprise@sparkjumbo.co.uk
W   www.sparkjumbo.co.uk

Estorick Collection [79]
39A Canonbury Square

London N1 2AN
T   7704 9522
F   7704 9531
E   curator@estorickcollection.com
W   www.estorickcollection.com

Euphorium Bakery [80]
203 Upper Street
London N1 1RQ
T   7704 6909
F   7704 6089

Eyre Brothers [145]
70 Leonard Street
London EC2A 4QX
T   7613 5346
F   7739 8199
W   www.eyrebrothers.co.uk

Fabric [75]
77A Charterhouse Street
London EC1M 3HN
T   7336 8898
F   7253 3932
W   www.fabriclondon.com

Fairuz [63]
3 Blandford Street
London W1H 3AA
T   7486 8108

Fandango [80]
50 Cross Street
London N1 2BA
T/F 7226 1777
E   shop@fandango.uk.com
W   www.fandango.uk.com

Faraday Museum [45]
21 Albemarle Street
London W1S 4BS
T   7409 2992
F   7629 3569
W   www.rigb.org/heritage

Fashion &Textile Museum [107]
83 Bermondsey Street
London SE1 3XF
T   7403 0222
F   7403 0555
E   info@ftmlondon.org
W   www.ftmlondon.org

Flow [20]
1–5 Needham Road
London W11 2RP
T   7243 0782
F   7792 1505
E   gallery.flow@ukgateway.net
W   www.flowgallery.co.uk

Fluid [75]
40 Charterhouse Street
London EC1M 6JN
T   7253 3444
F   7608 2777
E   info@fluidbar.com
W   www.fluidbar.com

The Foundry [91]
84–86 Great Eastern Street
London EC2A 3JL
T   7739 6900
W   www.foundry.tv

The Fountain Restaurant [46]
Fortnum & Mason
181 Piccadilly
London W1A 1ER
T   7973 4140
W   www.fortnumandmason.com

Frederick's [83]
106 Camden Passage
London N1 8EG
T   7359 2888
F   7359 5173
E   eat@fredericks.co.uk
W   www.fredericks.co.uk

French House [51]
49 Dean Street
London W1D 5BG
T   7437 2477
F   7287 9109

**Gallery 1930/Susie Cooper
Ceramics** [174]
18 Church Street
London NW8 8EP
T   7723 1555
F   7735 8309
E   gallery1930@aol.com
W   www.susiecooperceramics.com

Geffrye Museum [92]
Kingsland Road
London E2 3EA
T   7739 9893
F   7729 5647
E   info@geffrye-museum.org.uk
W   www.geffrye-museum.org.uk

Geo F. Trumper [45]
9 Curzon Street
London W1J 5HQ
T   7499 1850
E   enquiries@trumpers.com
W   www.trumpers.com

The George Inn [105]
77 Borough High Street
London SE1 1NH
T   7407 2056

Get Stuffed [80]
105 Essex Road
London N1 2SL
T   7226 1364
F   7359 8253
E   taxidermy@thegetstuffed.co.uk
W   www.thegetstuffed.co.uk

Ghost [175]
36 Ledbury Road
London W11 2AB
T   7229 1057
F   7792 9794
W   www.ghost.co.uk

Gill Wing Shops [80]
194–195 Upper Street
London N1 1RQ
T/F 7359 7697

Gina [38]
189 Sloane Street
London SW1X 9QR
T   7235 2932
F   7838 9720
W   www.ginashoes.com

Ginger [19]
115 Westbourne Grove
London W2 4UP
T   7908 1990
F   7908 1991

Globe Theatre [101]
21 New Globe Walk
Bankside
London SE1 9DT
T   7902 1400
F   7902 1401

E info@shakespearesglobe.com
W www.shakespeares-globe.org

Gordon's Wine Bar [151]
47 Villiers Street
London WC2N 6NE
T 7930 1408

Gotham Angels [80]
23 Islington Green
London N1 8DU
T 7359 8090
E info@gotham-angels.com
W www.gotham-angels.com

Great Eastern Dining Rooms [159]
54–56 Great Eastern Street
London EC2A 3QR
T 7613 4545
F 7613 4137
E info@greateasterndining.co.uk
W www.greateasterndining.co.uk

The Grill Room at the Dorchester [136]
53 Park Lane
London W1A 2HJ
T 7629 8888
F 7409 0114
E reservations@dorchesterhotel.com
W www.dorchesterhotel.com

The Guinea [46]
30 Bruton Place
London W1J 6NL
T 7499 1210

Hakkasan [133]
8 Hanway Place
London W1P 9DH
T 7907 1888
F 7907 1889
E mail@hakkasan.com

Harvie & Hudson [169]
97 Jermyn Street
London SW1Y 6JE
T 7839 3578
F 7839 7020
E info@harvieandhudson.com
W www.harvieandhudson.com

Hazlitt's [120]
6 Frith Street
Soho Square
London W1D 3JA
T 7434 1771
F 7439 1524
E reservations@hazlitts.co.uk
W www.hazlittshotel.com

Herbal Linea [90]
167 Brick Lane
London E2 7EE
T 07932 619 097
F 7254 4172
E info@herballinea.co.uk
W www.herballinea.co.uk

Home [133]
100–106 Leonard Street
London EC2A 4RH
T 7684 8618
F 7684 1491
W www.homebar.co.uk

Howarth Woodwind Specialists [64]
31–35 Chiltern Street
London W1U 7PN

T 7935 2407
F 7224 2564
E sales@howarth.uk.com
W www.howarth.uk.com

Hoxton Square Bar and Kitchen [159]
2–4 Hoxton Square
London N1 6NU
T 7613 0709

Hush [44]
8 Lancashire Court
London W1Y 9AD
T 7659 1500
F 7659 1501
W www.hush.co.uk

The Independence [80]
235 Upper Street
London N1 1RU
T 7704 6977

Institute of Contemporary Arts (ICA) [46]
The Mall
London SW1Y 5AH
T 7930 6393
W www.ica.org.uk

Isabell Kristensen [32]
33 Beauchamp Place
London SW3 1NU
T 7589 1798
F 7823 7703
W www.isabellkristensen.co.uk

Isola [155]
145 Knightsbridge
London SW1X 7PA
T 7838 1044

J. Floris [169]
89 Jermyn Street
London SW1Y 6JH
T 7930 2885
F 7930 1402
E fragrance@florislondon.com
W www.florislondon.com

J.J. Fox and Robert Lewis [46]
19 St James's Street
London SW1A 1ES
T 7930 3787
F 7495 0097
W www.jjfox.co.uk

The Jacksons [17]
5 All Saints Road
London W11 1HA
T 7792 8336
F 7792 5687
E enquiries@thejacksons.co.uk
W www.thejacksons.co.uk

Jamaica Wine House [89]
12 St Michael's Alley
London EC3V 9DS
T 7626 9496

James Smith and Son Umbrellas [67]
55 New Oxford Street
London WC1A 1BL
T 7836 4731
W www.james-smith.co.uk

Janet Reger [32]
2 Beauchamp Place
London SW3 1NG
T 7584 9368
F 7581 7946

E info@janetreger.com
W www.janetreger.co.uk

Jerusalem Tavern [83]
55 Britton Street
London EC1M 5NA
T 7490 4281

Jess James [51]
3 Newburgh Street
London W1F 7RE
T 7437 0199
F 7437 7001
E jess@jessjames.com
W www.jessjames.com

Jo Malone [39]
150 Sloane Street
London SW1X 9BX
T 7730 2100
E info@jomalone.co.uk
W www.jomalone.co.uk

John Lobb [162]
88 Jermyn Street
London SW1Y 6JD
T 7930 8089
F 7839 0981
E shop@johnlobb.com

Joie [63]
10 Museum Street
London WC1A 1JS
T/F 7497 5650

Julie's [18]
135 Portland Road
London W11 4LW
T 7727 7985
F 7229 4050
W www.juliesrestaurant.com

Junky [91]
12 Dray Walk
The Old Truman Brewery
91 Brick Lane
London E1 6RF
T 7247 1883
E junky.styling@virgin.net
W www.junkystyling.co.uk

The King's Head [80]
115 Upper Street
London N1 1QN
T 7226 1916
W www.kingsheadtheatre.org

Knightsbridge Hotel [116]
10 Beaufort Gardens
London SW3 1PT
T 7584 6300
F 7584 6355
E knightsbridge@firmdale.com
W www.knightsbridgehotel.com

Koh Samui [57]
65 Monmouth Street
London WC2 9DT
T 7240 4280
F 7240 3232

The Lamb [68]
94 Lamb's Conduit Street
London WC1N 3LZ
T 7405 0713

LASSCO St Michaels [94]
St Michael's Church
Mark Street
London EC2A 4ER
T 7749 9944
F 7749 9941

W st.michaels@lassco.co.uk
W www.lassco.co.uk

Le Taj [90]
134 Brick Lane
London E1 6RU
T 7247 4210
F 7377 6787
W www.letaj.co.uk

Leighton House [25]
12 Holland Park Road
London W14 8LZ
T 7602 3316
W www.rbkc.gov.uk/
  LHLeightonHouse

Le Pont de la Tour [102]
The Butlers Wharf Building
36d Shad Thames
London SE1 2YE
T 7403 8403
F 7403 0267
W www.conran-restaurants.com

Lesley Craze Gallery [75]
34 Clerkenwell Green
London EC1R 0DU
T 7608 0393
F 7251 5655
E lesleycraze@
  lesleycrazegallery.co.uk
W www.lesleycrazegallery.co.uk

Les Trois Garçons [94]
1 Club Row
London E1 6JX
T 7613 1924
F 7613 3067
E info@lestroisgarcons.com
W www.lestroisgarcons.com

Liberty [52]
214–220 Regent Street
London W1B 5AH
T 7734 1234
F 7573 9876
W www.liberty.co.uk

Lindsay House [135]
21 Romilly Street
London W1V 5TG
T 7439 0450
W www.lindsayhouse.co.uk

Liquid [159]
8 Pitfield Street
London N1 6HA
T 7729 0082

Liza Bruce [37]
9 Pont Street
London SW1X 9EJ
T 7235 8423

Lola's [83]
The Mall
359 Upper Street
London N1 0PD
T 7359 1932
E lolas@lolas.co.uk

London Eye [100]
Jubilee Gardens
London SE1 7BP
T 0870 5000 600
W www.londoneye.com

London Silver Vaults [68]
53–64 Chancery Lane
London WC2A 1QS
T 7242 3844

Lulu Guinness [38]
3 Ellis Street
London SW1X 9AL
T 7823 4828
F 7823 4889
W www.luluguinness.com

Maggie Jones [25]
6 Old Court Place
Kensington Church Street
London W8 4PL
T 7937 6462
F 7376 0510

Magma [57]
8 Earlham Street
London WC2H 9RY
T 7240 8498
E enquiries@magmabooks.com
W www.magmabooks.com

Maharishi [54]
19 Floral Street
London WC2E 9HL
T 7836 3860
F 7836 3857
E store@emaharishi.com
W www.emaharishi.com

The Mall [83]
359 Islington High Street
London N1 0PD

Manolo Blahnik [163]
49–51 Old Church Street
London SW3 5BS
T 7352 3863 or 7352 8622
F 7351 7314

Manor [17]
6–8 All Saints Road
London W11 1HH
T 7243 6363
E mail@manorw11.com

Map House [32]
54 Beauchamp Place
London SW3 1NY
T 7589 4325 or 7584 8559
F 7589 1041
E maps@themaphouse.com
W www.themaphouse.com

Marcus Campbell Art Books [107]
43 Holland Street
London SE1 9JR
T 7261 0111
E campbell@
marcuscampbell.demon.co.uk
W www.marcuscampbell.
demon.co.uk

Marx Memorial Library [75]
37a Clerkenwell Green
London EC1R 0DU
T 7253 1485
F 7251 6039
E marxlibrary@britishlibrary.net
W www.marxmemoriallibrary.
sageweb.co.uk

Match Bar [83]
45–47 Clerkenwell Road
London EC1M 5RS
T 7250 4002
W www.matchbar.com

Medicine Bar [159]
89 Great Eastern Street
London EC2A 3HX
T 7739 5173
F 7739 4996

E medicine@medicinebar.net
W www.medicinebar.net

Miller Harris [23]
14 Needham Road
London W11 2RP
T 7221 1545
F 7221 4370
E info@millerharris.com
W www.millerharris.com

Miller's Residence [128]
111a Westbourne Grove
London W2 4UW
T 7243 1024
F 7243 1064
E enquiries@millersuk.com
W www.millersuk.com

Mint [67]
70 Wigmore Street
London W1U 2SF
T 7224 4406
F 7224 4407
E info@mint-shop.co.uk

Mission [20]
45 Hereford Road
London W2 5AH
T 7792 4633

Momo [132]
25 Heddon Street
London W1B 4BH
T 7434 4040
F 7287 0404
E momoresto@aol.com

Moro [76]
34–36 Exmouth Market
London EC1R 4QE
T 7833 8336
F 7833 6338
E info@moro.co.uk

Neal's Yard Dairy [57]
17 Shorts Gardens
London WC2H 9UP
T 7240 5700
E mailorder@nealsyarddairy.co.uk

Neal's Yard Remedies [57]
15 Neal's Yard
London WC2H 9DP
T 7379 7222
F 7379 0705
W www.nealsyardremedies.com

Newman Arms [64]
23 Rathbone Street
London W1P 1NH
T 7636 1127
F 7580 5878

Nicole Farhi [48]
158 New Bond Street
London W1S 2UB
T 7499 8368
F 7499 7522
W www.nicolefarhi.com

Nigel Hall [54]
18 Floral Street
London WC2E 9DS
T 7836 8223
F 7379 3400

No. 5 Maddox Street [118]
5 Maddox Street
London W1S 2QD
T 7647 0200
F 7647 0300

E no5maddoxst@living-rooms.co.uk
W www.living-rooms.co.uk/
no5maddoxst

The Old Queens Head [80]
44 Essex Road
London N1 8LN
T 7354 9273

Overdose on Design [90]
182 Brick Lane
London E1 6SP
T/F 7613 1266
E shop@overdoseondesign.com
W www.overdoseondesign.com

Oxo Tower [100]
Bargehouse Street
London SE1 9PH
T 7803 3888
W www.oxotower.co.uk

Ozer [63]
4–5 Langham Place
Regent Street
London W1A 3DG
T 7323 0505
F 7323 0111

Ozwald Boateng [171]
9 Vigo Street
London W1X 1AL
T 7734 6868
F 7734 3737
E shop@bespokecoutureltd.co.uk

Paul Costelloe [32]
10 Beauchamp Place
London SW3 1NQ
T/F 7590 9902
W www.paulcostelloe.com

Paul Smith [164]
Westbourne House
122 Kensington Park Road
London W11 2EP
T 7727 3553

40–44 Floral Street [54]
London WC2E 9DS
T 7379 7133
W www.paulsmith.co.uk

Pauric Sweeney [94]
25a Pitfield Street
London N1 6HB
T/F 7253 5150

The Pelican [17]
45 All Saints Road
London W11 1HE
T 7792 3073
W www.singhboulton.co.uk/pelican

Penhaligon's [32]
18 Beauchamp Place
London SW3 1NQ
T 7584 4008
F 7584 4070
W www.penhaligons.co.uk

The Perseverance [68]
63 Lamb's Conduit Street
London WC1N 3NB
T 7405 8278
F 7831 0031

Philip Somerville [64]
38 Chiltern Street
London W1U 7QR
T 7224 1517
F 7486 5885

Philip Treacy [167]
69 Elizabeth Street
London SW1W 9PJ
T 7824 8787
F 7824 8262
W www.philiptreacy.co.uk

The Pineal Eye [53]
49 Broadwick Street
London W1F 9QR
T/F 7434 2567
W www.thepinealeye.com

Poetry Café [52]
22 Betterton Street
London WC2H 9BX
T 7420 9888
F 7240 4818
W www.poetrysociety.org.uk

Portobello Market [23]
Portobello Road
London W11

The Portrait [148]
The National Portrait Gallery
(top floor)
St Martin's Place
London WC2H 0HE
T 7312 2490
W www.npg.org.uk

Preem [90]
120 Brick Lane
London E1 6RL
T/F 7247 0397
W www.preembricklane.com

Preen [23]
Unit 5, Portobello Green Arcade
281 Portobello Road
London W10 5TZ
T 8968 1542

Puppy [23]
26 Portobello Green
London W10 5TZ
T/F 8964 1547
E service@puppy-bedstock.co.uk
W www.puppy-bedstock.co.uk

Quality Chop House [76]
92–94 Farringdon Road
London EC1R 3EA
T 7837 5093
F 7833 8748
E thequalitychophouse@
claranet.com

R. K. Stanley's [64]
6 Little Portland Street
London W1W 7JE
T 7462 0099
F 7462 0088

Rachel Riley [37]
14 Pont Street
London SW1X 9EN
T 7935 7007
F 7935 7004
E enquiries@rachelriley.com
W www.rachelriley.com

The Red Fort [142]
77 Dean Street
London W1D 3SH
T 7437 2525
F 7434 0721
E info@redfort.co.uk
W www.redfort.co.uk

Rellik [174]
8 Golborne Road

London W10 5NW
T/F 8962 0089

Richard James [165]
29 Savile Row
London W1X 1AF
T 7434 0605
F 7287 2265
E mail@richardjames.co.uk
W www.richardjames.co.uk

Ronnie Scott's [52]
47 Frith Street
London W1D 4HT
T 7439 0747
F 7437 5081
E ronniescotts@ronniescotts.co.uk
W www.ronniescotts.co.uk

The Rookery [112]
Peter's Lane
Cowcross Street
London EC1M 6DS
T 7336 0931
F 7336 0932
E reservations@rookery.co.uk
W www.rookery.co.uk

**Royal Institute of British Artists
(RIBA)** [63]
66 Portland Place
London W1B 1AD
T 7580 5533
F 7255 1541
E info@inst.riba.org
W www.architecture.com

Royal Opera House [54]
Covent Garden
London WC2E 9DD
Box Office:
T 7304 4000
F 7212 9460
Restaurant reservations:
T 7212 9254
F 7212 9239
E searcys@roh.org.uk
W www.royalopera.org

Ruby Lounge [157]
33 Caledonian Road
London N1 9BU
T 7837 9558
W www.ruby.uk.com

Rules [134]
35 Maiden Lane
London WC2E 7LB
T 7836 5314
F 7497 1081
E info@rules.co.uk
W www.rules.co.uk

Sadler's Wells [77]
Rosebery Avenue
London EC1R 4TN
T 7863 8198
F 7863 8199
E reception@sadlerswells.com
W www.sadlerswells.com

The Sanctuary [54]
12 Floral Street
London WC2E 9DH
T 0870 770 3350
F 0870 770 3359
E info@thesanctuary.co.uk
W www.thesanctuary.co.uk

The Sanderson [114]
50 Berners Street
London W1T 3NG
T 7300 1400

F 7300 1401
E sanderson@
ianschragerhotels.com
W www.ianschragerhotels.com

The Scarsdale Tavern [25]
23A Edwardes Square
London W8 6HE
T 7937 1811
F 7938 2986

Selfridges [168]
400 Oxford Street
London W1A 1AB
T 08708 377 377
W www.selfridges.co.uk

Serpentine Gallery [39]
Kensington Gardens
London W2 3XA
T 7298 1515
W www.serpentinegallery.org

Sharp Eye [51]
2 Ganton Street
London W1V 1LJ
T 7137 7916

Simon Finch [24]
61a Ledbury Road
London W11 2AL
T 7792 3303
F 7243 2134
W www.simonfinch.com

Sir John Soane's Museum [68]
13 Lincoln's Inn Fields
London WC2A 3BP
T 7405 2107
F 7831 8957
W www.soane.org

Sketch [140]
9 Conduit Street
London W1S 2XZ
T 0870 777 4488
F 0870 777 4400

Smiths of Smithfield [141]
67–77 Charterhouse Street
London EC1M 6HJ
T 7251 7950
E reservations@
smithsofsmithfield.co.uk
W www.smithsofsmithfield.co.uk

Smithy's [150]
15–17 Leeke Street
London WC1X 9HZ
T 7278 5949
F 7837 6898

The Social [167]
5 Little Portland Street
London WC1N 5AG
T 7434 0620
F 7636 4993
W www.thesocial.co.uk

Solange Azagury-Partridge [167]
171 Westbourne Grove
London W11 2RS
T 7792 0197

Somerset House [57]
The Strand
London WC2R 1LA
T 7845 4600
E info@somerset-house.org.uk
W www.somerset-house.org.uk

Sotheran's [49]
2–5 Sackville Street

London W1X 2DP
T 7439 6151
F 7434 2019
E sotherans@sotherans.co.uk
W www.sotherans.co.uk

**South Bank Centre/
People's Palace** [102]
South Bank
London
T 7921 0600
F 7928 0063
W www.sbc.org.uk

Southwark Cathedral [107]
Montague Close
London SE1 9DA
T 7367 6700
F 7367 6725
E cathedral@dswark.org.uk
W www.dswark.org/cathedral

Space Boudoir [20]
214 Westbourne Grove
London W11 2RH
T 7229 6533
W www.spaceboudoir.com

Spitalfields Market [93]
Commercial Street
London E1
W www.spitalfields.org.uk
Open Monday to Friday,
9:00–5:00; Sundays 9:30–5:30

St Bartholomew the Great [74]
West Smithfield
London EC1A 7JQ
T 7606 5171
F 7600 6909
E st.bartholomew@btinternet.com
W www.greatstbarts.com

St Etheldreda [68]
Ely Place
London EC1N 6RY

St John [144]
26 St John Street
London EC1M 4AY
T 7251 0848
F 7251 4090
W www.stjohnrestaurant.co.uk

St Stephen Walbrook [89]
Walbrook Street
London EC4

Stephen Einhorn [80]
210 Upper Street
London N1 1RL
T 7359 4977
F 7354 0953
E info@stepheneinhorn.co.uk
W www.stepheneinhorn.co.uk

Suzy Harper [80]
44 Cross Street
London N1 2BA
T 7288 0820

Tanner Krolle [170]
1 Burlington Gardens
London W1S 3EW
T 7287 5121
F 7287 1606
W www.tannerkrolle.com

Tadema Gallery [83]
10 Charlton Place
Camden Passage
London N1 8AJ

T/F 7359 1055
E info@tademagallery.com
W www.tademagallery.com

Target Gallery [67]
7 Windmill Street
London W1T 2JE
T 7636 6295

Tate Modern [104]
Bankside
London SE1 9TG
T 7887 8000
W www.tate.org.uk/modern

Tatty Devine [90]
236 Brick Lane
London E2 7EB
T 7739 9009
E info@tattydevine.com
W www.tattydevine.com

Threadneedles [122]
5 Threadneedle Street
London EC2R 8AY
T 7657 8080
F 7657 8100
E restthreadneedles@
theetongroup.com
W www.etontownhouse.com

Three Kings [79]
7 Clerkenwell Close
Off Clerkenwell Green
London EC1R 0DY
T 7253 0483

Townhouse [32]
31 Beauchamp Place
London SW3 1NU
T 7589 5080
F 7581 3777
E emails@lab-townhouse.com
W www.lab-townhouse.com

Tribe [80]
52 Cross Street
London N1 2BA
T 7226 5544
E derek@tribe-london.com
W www.tribe-london.com

Trudy Hanson [17]
25 All Saints Road
London W11 1HE
T 7792 1300
W www.trudyhanson.co.uk

The Truman Brewery [91]
91–95 Brick Lane
London E1 6QL
W www.trumanbrewery.com

Turnbull & Asser [169]
71–72 Jermyn Street
London SW1Y 6PF
T 7808 3000
F 7808 3001
W www.turnballandasser.co.uk

Twenty Twenty-one [80]
274 Upper Street
London N1 2UA
T/F 7288 1996
W www.twentytwentyone.com

Uli [17]
16 All Saints Road
London W11 1HH
T 7727 7511

Under the Westway [156]
Westbourne Studios

242 Acklam Road
London W10 5JJ
T   7575 3123
F   7575 3124

Unto This Last [90]
230 Brick Lane
London E2
E   Comments@UntoThisLast.co.uk
W   www.UntoThisLast.co.uk

V. V. Rouleaux [35]
54 Sloane Square
Cliveden Place
London SW1W 8AW
T   7730 3125
F   7730 9985
E   sloane@vvrouleaux.com
W   www.vvrouleaux.com

Vertigo⁴² [151]
Tower 42
25 Old Broad Street
London EC2N 1HQ
T   7877 7842
F   7877 7788
W   www.vertigo42.co.uk

Vessel [19]
114 Kensington Park Road
London W11 2PW
T   7727 8001
E   vesselstore@aol.com

The Vestry [89]
All Hallows by the Tower
Byward Street
London EC3R 5BJ
T   7977 6899
F   7481 5300
E   info@the-vestry.com
W   www.the-vestry.com

Vibe Bar [90]
The Old Truman Brewery
91–95 Brick Lane
London E1 6QL
T   7377 2899

Victoria and Albert Museum [30]
Cromwell Road
London SW7 2RL
T   7942 2000
E   vanda@vam.ac.uk
W   www.vam.ac.uk

Viet Hoa [89]
70–72 Kingsland Road
London E2 8DP
T   7729 8293

Villandry [64]
170 Great Portland Street
London W1W 5QB
T   7631 3131
F   7631 3030
W   www.villandry.com

Vinopolis [107]
1 Bank End
London SE1 9BU
T   0870 4444 777
E   sales@vinopolis.co.uk
W   www.vinopolis.co.uk

The Vintage House [50]
42 Old Compton Street
London W1V 6LR
T   7437 5112
W   www.sohowhisky.com

Virginia [18]
98 Portland Road

Clarendon Cross
London W11 4LQ
T   7727 9908

Wall [18]
1 Denbigh Road
London W11 2SJ
T   7243 4623
F   7243 4622

The Wallace Collection [64]
Manchester Square
London W1U 3BN
T   7563 9500
F   7224 2155
E   admin@the-wallace-
    collection.org.uk
W   www.the-wallace-collection.org.uk

West Street [126]
13–15 West Street
London WC2H 9NE
T   7010 8600,
    dinner reservations: 7010 8700
F   7010 8600
E   weststreet@egami.co.uk
W   www.weststreet.org

The Westbourne [20]
101 Westbourne Park Villas
London W2 5ED
T   7221 1332
F   7243 8081
W   www.thewestbourne.com

White Cube [89]
48 Hoxton Square
London N1 6PB
T   7930 5373
F   7749 7470
W   www.whitecube.com

Whitechapel Art Gallery [92]
80–82 Whitechapel High Street
London E1 7QX
T   7522 7878
F   7377 1685
E   info@whitechapel.org
W   www.whitechapel.org

Wild at Heart [24]
49a Ledbury Road
London W11 2AA
T   7727 3095

William Hunt [165]
41 Savile Row
London W1S 3QQ
T/F 7439 1921

William Yeoward Crystal [30]
336 King's Road
London SW3 5UR
T   7351 5454
F   7351 9469
W   www.williamyeowardcrystal.com

Windsor Castle [155]
114 Campden Hill Road
London W8 7AR
T   7243 9551
W   www.windsor-castle-pub.com

Wink [94]
105 Great Eastern Street
London EC2A 3JD
T   7608 2323
F   7608 1222

Ye Olde Mitre Tavern [152]
1 Ely Place
Ely Court

London EC1N 6SJ
T   7405 4751

Zaika [143]
1 Kensington High Street
London W8 5SF
T   7795 6533
F   7937 8854
E   info@zaika-restaurant.co.uk
W   www.zaika-restaurant.co.uk

Zarvis [23]
4 Portobello Green
281 Portobello Road
London W10 5TZ
T/F 8968 5435
E   v.zarvis@virgin.net
W   www.zarvis.com

Zig Zag [17]
12 All Saints Road
London W11 1HH
T   7243 2008

BRIGHTON [178]
*Direct trains to Brighton leave
approximately every half hour from
King's Cross Thameslink, London
Bridge (1 hour and 20 minutes) and
Victoria stations (50 minutes). (From
London call 08457 48 49 50 or check
www.railtrack.co.uk for specific times.)
Both hotels and most destinations in
Brighton are walking distance from the
station; taxis are plentiful.*

Blanch House
17 Atlingworth Street
Brighton
East Sussex BN2 1PL
T   01273 603504
F   01273 689813
W   www.blanchhouse.co.uk
Rooms from £100

Hotel Pelirocco
10 Regency Square
Brighton
East Sussex BN1 2FG
T   01273 327055
F   01273 733845
W   www.hotelpelirocco.co.uk
Rooms from £100

BATH [180]
*Fast trains to Bath leave every hour
(from London call 08457 48 49 50 or
check www.railtrack.co.uk for specific
times); from Paddington Station the
trip takes 1 hour and 20 minutes.
Babington House is approximately
12 miles from Bath. The easiest way
of reaching the hotel is by taxi; the fare
is £25 to £30.*

Babington House
Babington
Nr Frome
Somerset BA11 3RW
T   01373 812266
F   01373 812112
E   enquiries@babingtonhouse.co.uk
W   www.babingtonhouse.co.uk
Rooms from £210

BRAY [182]
*The 30- to 40-minute train journey to
Maidenhead leaves approximately every
half hour from Paddington Station
(from London call 08457 48 49 50 or
check www.railtrack.co.uk for specific
times). Take a taxi from Maidenhead*

*station to Bray High Street or directly to
any of the destinations below; fares are
about £10.*

Monkey Island Hotel
Bray-on-Thames
Berkshire SL6 2EE
T   01628 623 400
F   01628 784 732
E   monkeyisland@btconnect.com
W   www.methotels.com/
    monkeyisland
Rooms from £200

The Fat Duck
High Street
Bray-on-Thames
Berkshire SL6 2AQ
T   01628 580 333
F   01628 776 188
W   www.fatduck.co.uk

The Waterside Inn
Ferry Road
Bray-on-Thames
Berkshire
SL6 2AT
T   01628 620 691
F   01628 784 710
W   www.waterside-inn.co.uk
Rooms from £160

GRAVETYE MANOR [184]
*Take the 50-minute train ride from
London Victoria to East Grinstead;
trains leave every half hour from
London call 08457 48 49 50 or check
www.railtrack.co.uk for specific times).
From the station, take a taxi to the
hotel; the fare is about £15.*

Nr East Grinstead
West Sussex RH19 4LJ
T   01342 810567
F   01342 810080
E   info@gravetyemanor.co.uk
W   www.gravetyemanor.co.uk
Rooms from £190